To Jack Garden -

*though no longer with us,
his spirit lives on in
these pages.*

Pigeon Spire - J.F. Garden.

*Page 2-3
John Simpson in a chimney on Snowpatch -
Tom Egan Memorial Route:
Photo by Daryl Hatten*

THE BUGABOOS

AN ALPINE HISTORY

By J.F. Garden

The Bugaboos
An Alpine History

John F. Garden
Footprint Publishing
Revelstoke, BC

Photographs by: Glen Boles
Ed Cooper
Scott Flavelle
J.F. Garden
Byron Harmon
(Archives of the
Canadian Rockies)
Daryl Hatten
Roger W. Laurilla
James B. Maitre
Rob Rohn
John Simpson
Uldis Veideman
Jim Weston

Illustrations by: Glen Boles
Dan Graydon

Design and layout by Catherine Garden

Editor, Penny Graham

Typing, Shirley Magus

Printed in Hong Kong by
Overseas Printing Corporation

Typesetting by Walford & Foy

Published by: Footprint Publishing Co. Ltd.
Box 1830
Revelstoke, BC   V0E 2S0

©J.F. Garden, 1987

ISBN 0-9691621-1-1

Garden, J.F. (John Franklin), 1948-
The Bugaboos : an alpine history

Bibliography: p. 152,155

1. Bugaboos, The (B.C.) – History.
2. Mountaineering – British Columbia –
Bugaboos,The – History.   I. Title.

FC3845.B94G37 1987   971.1'45   C86-090245-5
F1089.B94G37 1987

Anniversary Peak and Marmolata at dusk - J.F. Garden

Pigeon Spire and the Howsers - J.F. Garden

Mountain Fireweed - J.F. Garden

CONTENTS

Pigeon Spire, north face – Dan Graydon

A vertical mosaic - Howser Towers - J.F. Garden

ACKNOWLEDGEMENT

The Bugaboos have always been a mystical place for me. To have the opportunity of assembling the illustrations and stories which compose this book, and then to see the end result published is somewhat mystical for me as well. No one will ever be able to completely do justice to such a beautiful place with either photographs or descriptive prose, but hopefully our efforts will at least reflect some of the grand alpine feeling that these special mountains evince.

In order to complete this volume on the Bugaboos, I have relied on the talents of many people: photographers, writers, artists, climbers and nature lovers. The whole idea of a Bugaboo book was broached some years ago when I was trying to find a publisher for The Selkirks – Nelson's Mountains, our first and so far very successful book.

I had approached, among others, The Seattle Mountaineers, to publish the Selkirk book. At that time John Pollack, now of Alpen Books, our U.S.A. distributor, was the man to talk to at "The Mountaineers." He wasted no time in turning me away from The Mountaineers, but at the same time suggested that somebody should do something on the Bugaboos – an idea that immediately took root.

Then it was a matter of assembling the material, largely photographs and stories. At the Peter and Catherine Whyte Foundation, Archives of the Canadian Rockies in Banff, Alberta, I was able to glean a great deal of information on past climbs, as well as old photographs of the Bugaboos. The journals of the American and Canadian Alpine Club provided much needed information and Edward Cavell, photographic curator, was able to assist in discovering photographs of past years in the Bugaboos; most taken by the famous Byron Harmon.

Past climbs were well documented and early photographs were available, but what about contemporary material? Climbers tend to be somewhat humble about their exploits, as they are usually out for enjoyment and not publicity. So, it was with great appreciation that people such as Scott Flavell, Rob Rohn, and John Simpson provided written accounts and photographs to round out this Bugaboo book. Together with the photographs of Uldis Veideman, Glen Boles, Roger W. Laurilla, James B. Maitre, Jim Weston, Ed Cooper and myself, we hope we have been able to portray the moods and scenes of the Bugaboo Spires.

Then there are those whose deep interests in mountaineering provoked them to answer in the affirmative when I asked them to review the manuscript. Hans and Margaret Gmoser, William L. Putnam, Leonard and Joan-Mary Mason and Fred Beckey unselfishly gave of their time to help ensure not only a readable manuscript, but one as free of errors as possible. Special appreciation goes to Fred Beckey, one of North America's great mountaineers, for his introduction to the Bugaboos and for his undying interest in our project.

One of the special features of this Bugaboo book is the artwork we have reproduced here with the permission of Glen Boles and Dan Graydon. Glen is one of the most enthusiastic mountaineers I have ever met, and he and his wife Liz are two of the greatest of people. His art is the work of one who has intimate feeling for his subject and hopefully in the future we may see a volume of Glen's work on its own. Dan Graydon is a young and upcoming artist whose interests span many realms, but his feelings for the Bugaboos have a depth that reflect a night we bivouaced on Snowpatch, when sleep was impossible because of an incredible display of "Northern Lights" amongst the spires.

In order to produce this book and prepare the manuscript and photographs for the printer, three ladies are of paramount importance. Shirley Magus was responsible for the typing involved, unendingly revising the manuscript in preparation for typeset. Penny Graham took that manuscript and pored over it pointing out the flaws and discrepancies which tend to run amok in an author's disregard for the English language. Finally and most important of all, the final layout and artwork had to be done so that the printer could reproduce what we desired. This was the greatest task of all, but Catherine Garden was well up to it and in fact bothered me incessantly to get on with it. To her, such projects are a work of love and the results show it.

There are bound to be some errors and omissions in a work of this nature. There are undoubtably other stories of importance to the Bugaboos that have been either overlooked or that I am unaware of. It would be impossible to include every story and detail, even should I have access to them all.

Hopefully I have not overlooked anyone whose efforts have gone into this book. There are of course, countless other people who help in ways indirectly associated with such a project as this. These people are my friends and family and fellow photographers. My friend Dusty and my father especially, are two who bear much responsibility for setting me off on my merry way; and Trudy Golley-Silano deserves much thanks for providing us with a showplace for our literary and photographic efforts. Thanks too must go to the people of Revelstoke, British Columbia, who have proudly taken us in and supported us immensely. They know how special it is to live in the shadow of nature's greatest wonders.

Climbers on Crescent Spire - Glen Boles

PROLOGUE

Ambitions of adventure have been the catalyst for many of the world's events and discoveries. To climb and explore; to push into new frontiers and gain new heights: these are the ambitions of certain men.

Those men, mountaineers, rock and ice climbers, are forever exploring regions, scaling unclimbed peaks and pioneering new and untried routes.

Whether such ambitions of adventure are considered irrational objectives or sane ideas, it matters not to the climber. Essentially, society neither rules the values of the mountaineer nor restricts him. In the natural domain, he is beyond the boundary of society, restricted solely by personal limits or the objective dangers posed by nature.

Though often ignored in our modern civilization, nature still exerts tremendous influence on our lives. With violent geologic events, erratic weather and baffling climatic changes, our world remains wracked by the forces which created it. Defeated only by those natural forces, man seeks to discover the link between himself and nature. The answers may be found, so some men believe, in direct confrontation with nature. The outcome of such confrontations often provides satisfaction and stirs feelings of supremacy over the elements. The mountaineer's success against the odds of nature builds egos, his failure can bring grave misgivings.

Nature is an unforgiving foe. The elements can be terribly unrelenting. Death can be instantaneous or slow and painful. Even the best of men often succumb to nature's fury. Fleeting moments of supremacy may be gained but the humbling aspects of nature will deflate any swollen ego, or thoughts of immortality. Even mountaineers remain mere mortals!

The land, which predates man, is the stage upon which nature plays out everyday dramas. With the evolution of the planet the physical features of the Earth's crust have been generated. The location, composition, shape and height of mountains, the crust's most glaring irregularities, are the result of so many unpredictable geological events that one

tends to believe that nature's only principle is uncontrolled chaos. Though the processes of nature are known and understood, the driving forces behind the events remain mysterious.

The granitic spires of the Bugaboo mountains adhere to those chaotic rules of nature. Their rock formations are quite understood but why they should exist in the southern Interior Ranges of British Columbia is a question answerable only in the global context of the theories of continental drift. Why the Bugaboos should be of such magnificent stature and beauty is a precept determined by a chance series of events, repetitive throughout geologic history, but never resulting in similar landforms.

Geologically, the Bugaboos are largely made up of crystalline quartz monzonite rock of the Cretaceous era in the geologic time scale; that is 65 to 135 million years old. This 70 million year period is a good indication of the time span required for the elements of quartz monzonite to crystallize into rock from its original state of molten magma.

Originating from deep within the Earth's core, the hot, fluid magma was forced up through cracks and weak fissures in the earth's crust from below the ancient pre-existing Purcell Mountains; a range which was already in existence and perhaps yet rising during the Cretaceous era. Why or when this event took place in the particular location it did is subject to much conjecture, but in all likelihood it was concurrent with great upheavals in the earth's crust occurring at the time, perhaps even concurrent with the great heaving and thrusting that created the Rocky Mountains which now lie to the east of the Purcells. As the molten rock flowed into the bowels of the older Purcells, the land was wracked with earthquakes producing faults and fractures. The super-heated rock raced into those fissures and weaknesses, often altering the old rock and sometimes producing rich mineral veins and pockets.

The Purcell Mountains were composed of sedimentary rocks from the Pre-Cambrian period of geologic time, 600 million years ago and were pushed up perhaps 400 million years later. Follow-

ing the intrusion of the molten rock, which was to become the Bugaboo granites, 65 million years of erosion reduced the high peaks and overburden of the Purcells exposing the rocks that lay within. Removal of the softer sedimentary rock left harder formations of crystallized quartz monzonite granite standing in relief against surrounding weaker Purcell rock.

In geologic time, the Bugaboos are considered a recent development. Compared with the total history of our planet, these mountains have only existed for a brief time. The appearance of modern man in the environs of the Bugaboos is such a minutely recent occurrence, it may seem not to warrant any consideration at all. Even compared to civilization's existence on the Earth, the appearance of men in the Bugaboo wilderness is only a very modern development. Certainly, Canada was long established as a nation when the first recorded exploration of the Bugaboos took place.

Previously visited perhaps by native Indians, or prospectors and trappers, the Bugaboos remained a desolate wilderness until adventurers dedicated to the discovery of unconquered mountains forged their way into the area during the summer of 1910. These men were the first to enter the area on an expedition of exploration rather than one of exploitation for economic reasons.

Theirs was a distinct and momentous journey which they undertook to an area where mountain peaks remained unclimbed, perhaps unseen.

Theirs was an adventure into the realm of nature untouched, of beauty unspoiled – the dream of all mountaineers!

THE BUGABOOS

Bugaboo Glacier and the Nunataks — U. Veideman

Map Illustrations — Thom Nelson

LEGEND

⚒ Mine

▬▬ Road to Bugaboo Lodge

▬ ▬ Trail to Bugaboo Pass

▬▬ Bugaboo Glacier Provincial Park

Bugaboo Pass

Bugaboo Creek

Frenchm
Mounta

INTRODUCTION

The Bugaboos have become the quintessential tag among North America's mountains. As grand cathedrals of granitic rock set among glistening glaciers, they seemingly defy comparison. It could be said the Bugaboos were deliberately shaped by the Creator to stun man's eye, to be the theme of a dream. Certainly they have the foundation for a fantasy.

All alpine mountain groups have something special to render them picturesque, scenic, grand, even majestic. But the Bugaboos have a classic majesty formed by elements of granite and ice, and sculptured by timeless processes to forms that seem to soar into the heavens. In fact, one could well imagine them to be the earthly haven of celestial gods.

These forms of nature which can so inspire us, and at times almost seem supernatural, stand as monuments that challenge the endless processes of weathering and natural destruction. The land and the life it supports is constantly changing. Some day these spires of rock, like the highest summit in the Sierra Nevada, which Clarence King called "A great monolith left standing amid the ruins of a bygone geological empire," will no longer frame the skyline. But during man's day on Earth, geologic forces will not humble the Bugaboos.

After their discovery, it required some time for man to locate the unique cluster of rock spires in the Purcell Range that first took the name "The Nunataks" after that historic and pioneering British-Canadian venture in 1910 by Longstaff and party. Who knows what the early miners and trappers of the region called the spires, or even thought of them, but it was a frustration in the search for riches that provided a metaphor — a word which fitted the spire Conrad Kain returned to climb in 1916. Kain sought others to share his joy in the discovery of these mammoth, closely-standing, sharp-edged rock forms. For years few ventured to this distant, lonely mountain kingdom west of the upper Columbia River. But in time the human element took importance. It was only logical that these spires would entice adventurous alpinists who had visited the Rocky Mountains, but sought new personal challenge. The Rockies, with their often massive pyramidal forms, were now well explored. The Bugaboos promised a new romance, and they promised firm, soaring rock.

Today's Bugaboos, yesterday's "Nunataks," surrounded by glaciers, have become one of Canada's wonderful, all-season mountain playgrounds, one that has become renowned even in other lands. Those who have visited the Bugaboos, or even admired the spectacular photographic images of these natural cathedrals presented in this book, have received some benefit from their existence. These rewards have often been rich. It is important that those who visit and manage this special region keep it unchanged.

John Garden's book is a beautiful, moving portrayal of these majestic Canadian peaks – not only in the historical context of those who sought them – but in their ecological setting. Here is a sensitive feeling for the environment, one which we all have a responsibility to preserve in a natural state. Garden's book, in a sense, is a perceptive tribute to the human adventures forged among and on the spires. It is a dedication to Conrad Kain, and as the author has written: "The man is gone but the legacy remains, entwined in the history of Canada's mountains..."

Fred Beckey

British Columbia

Prince Rupert

Rocky Mountains

Alberta

Coast Mountains

Prince George

Edmonton

Kamloops

Selkirk Mountains

Purcell Mountains

Golden

Banff

Vancouver

Revelstoke

Vernon

Kelowna

Calgary

Penticton

Nelson

Monashee Mountains

Cranbrook

Lethbridge

Seattle

Washington

Spokane

Montana

Idaho

Area Blow-up
Pages 16 - 17

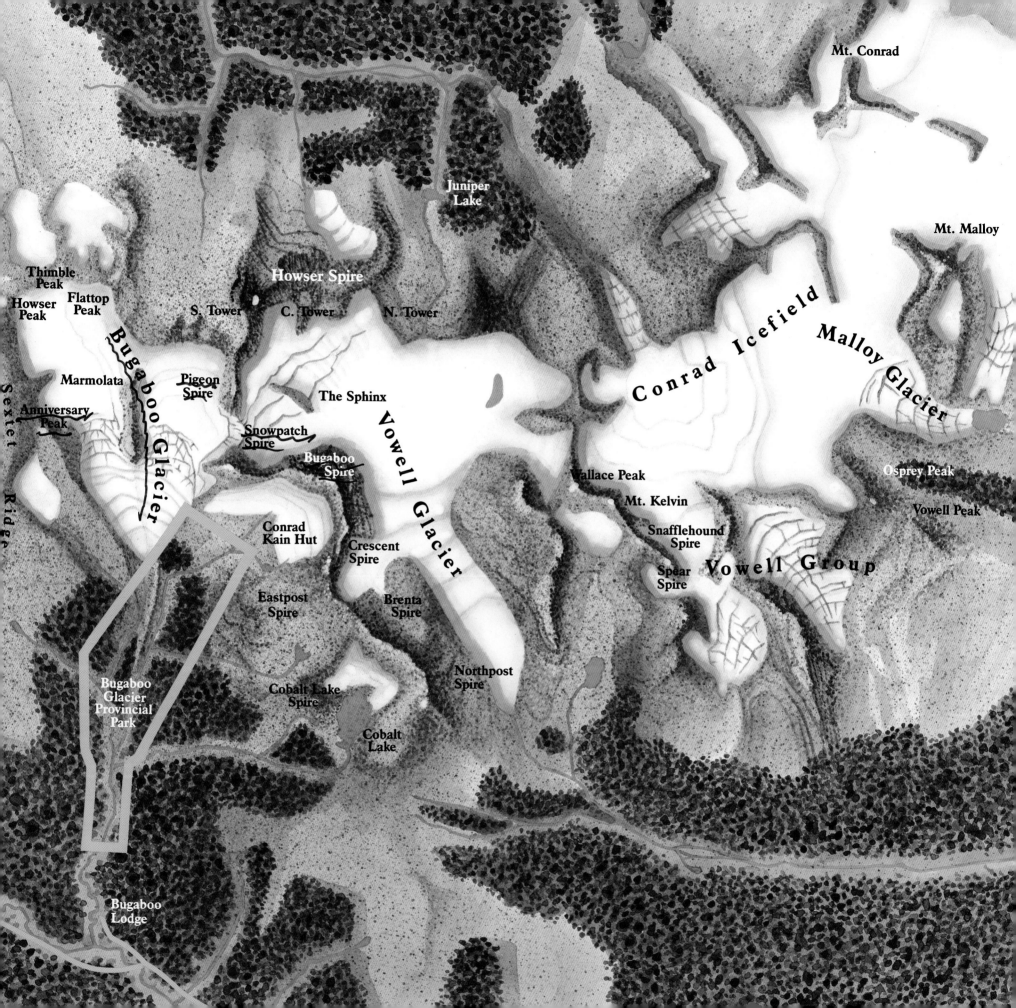

Conrad Kain-guide, 1910 - Archives of the Canadian Rockies

PART I:
CONRAD KAIN

Born in Austria on August 10, 1883, in the small village of Nasswald, Conrad Kain was to become Canada's most famous guide and mountaineer.

After a very difficult early life, Conrad chose to guide hunters and climbers on and around the Raxalpe which overshadowed his home. The choice was forced upon him as no one wanted to employ Conrad because of his frequent absences from previous jobs; absences due to his love of climbing. The Raxalpe was a popular climbing area of the Viennese, and so Conrad was able to garner many important clients of means. These people employed him for many years on climbs throughout the Alps, enabling Conrad to establish his reputation and attain a very high degree of respect, as well as his FuhrerBüch authorizing him to act as a professional guide.

In time the Alps became too small for Conrad Kain, and he yearned for the chance of wealth and adventure which other lands promised. Encouraged by his longtime client Dr. Erich Pistor, Conrad chose Canada as his destiny. The Canadian Pacific Railway was at that time hiring mountain guides for their resorts in the Canadian Rockies. Much to Conrad's disappointment Swiss guides from Interlaken were chosen. However, Conrad was put in touch with Arthur Wheeler of the Alpine Club of Canada, who was also a surveyor for the Dominion Government. As Wheeler's assistant and guide, in both surveying and at the Alpine Club of Canada's annual summer camp, Conrad gained a great reputation and many first ascents in the little explored Canadian Rockies.

The occupation of mountain guide is a seasonal job at best. The long Canadian winters forced Kain to take up various occupations including working as a farmhand and a trapper. Though he enjoyed trapping he found that life to be very hard, and therefore during the winter of 1913 he decided to travel. In Australia and New Zealand the seasons are reversed from those of Canada, and he climbed in New Zealand's Southern Alps. For many seasons thereafter he travelled between Canada and New Zealand guiding in both countries, taking advantage of the climbing season in two hemispheres.

1913 heralded Conrad's most famous climb, that of the first certain ascent of Mt. Robson with Albert MacCarthy and Bill Foster. From that summer on Conrad was always in demand and in fact he and MacCarthy formed a long-lasting friendship which took them on many great adventures including those in the Bugaboos.

Pigeon Spire in mists — U. Veideman

271. A DAY'S HUNT. THREE GRIZZLIES.

*A.O. Wheeler and T.G. Longstaff with three dead grizzlies.
'Longstaff-Wheeler' Bugaboo Expedition, 1910 - Archives of the
Canadian Rockies, photo by Byron Harmon*

CHAPTER ONE:
The Nunataks

A cool breeze wafted down over the warm meadows and rustled the leaves of the heavily-laden huckleberry bushes. A mountain stream tumbled and fell, washing the banks on which the ripe branches hung. Amid the sounds of tumbling waters and rustling leaves, a low contented groaning noise rose and fell on the wind.

Wandering in the meadow grasses and huckleberry bushes, an old sow grizzly led her two offspring foraging in this abundance of nature. Fall was in the air and the bears were gaining winter layers of fat, eating anything that suited their palate. Curiously poking and digging in the bushes, the bears were unaware of the presence of another mammal on the edge of the meadow.

Suddenly a shot rang out! The old sow buckled to the ground. A figure sprang out from behind a boulder. A rifle was aimed at the first of the sow's offspring but before another shot was released, Tom Longstaff found an enraged and wounded female grizzly bear charging directly at him.

Another shot – the snarling bear loomed larger. A third shot, and she crumpled bloodily to the ground. Only yards behind her was one of the two-year old cubs. One clean shot dispatched that one. Then much to Longstaff's horror, the second cub, of sizeable proportions and with porcupine quills in his nose, charged. With two quick and extremely lucky shots the bear fell within feet of him. Shaken and tired from the sudden rush of adrenalin which accompanied the incident, Longstaff made his way back to camp. He quietly sat down to relax and asked if he could get help on the morrow to recover his game. Conrad Kain asked if he had shot a goat.

"No," Longstaff had replied, "three grizzlies."

Dr. Thomas George Longstaff, physiologist, Himalayan and Arctic explorer, renowned hunter and author, later wrote of his encounter with the bears.

". . .The result was far more appalling than all six tigers I had met put together."[1]

Longstaff entered the wilderness Purcell Mountains in an effort to traverse them overland to Kootenay Lake. He was accompanied by outfit-ters Charlie Lawrence and Bert Barrow, famed photographer Byron Harmon of Banff, Dominion surveyor Arthur Oliver Wheeler and guide Conrad Kain. A.O. Wheeler was to survey the region for the Dominion Government. His survey would establish high altitude triangulation stations and possibly complete some first ascents with the help of guide and companion Conrad Kain.

Long referred to as the Spillimacheen Spires, visible from various high peaks in the Rockies, the Bugaboos were a great curiosity to climbers and explorers. At this time, the only people who knew anything of the Bugaboos were prospectors who had combed the mountains in search of gold. On the morning of August 30, 1910, the sun rose over the Rockies casting light on the mists of the Columbia River and the wake of the steamer "Klahowya." Longstaff, Wheeler and party set off determined to explore those spires, and to record their position and existence on the maps of North America.

A trail was known to have been cut along Bugaboo Creek by miners and in fact a small rush had occurred in the area in 1906. Disembarking at Haffner's Landing on the west bank of the Columbia, the party assembled the pack train and set out on their exploration. It was known that this route was once used to cross the Purcells by one Mr. Wilmer C. Wells[2] and another pioneer during the winter of 1898. Whether this route would lead them to the Spires was unknown.

Striking out in fine late summer weather the trail was followed easily, passing to the south of the lower canyon of the Spillimacheen River then westward along the north bank of the Bugaboo Creek. The party struggled for three days over an increasingly overgrown trail, through burnt and fallen timber and past a still smouldering forest fire. While Wheeler established the first of his ten survey stations in the area, Byron Harmon went up the valley to clear a trail for the horses. In the evening he returned, overjoyed at having found a "remarkably fine" glacier at the head of the north fork of the Bugaboo Creek.[3] Around the campfire that night there was spirited discussion as Wheeler and Kain had seen from their first survey station, wrote Longstaff, "the upper reaches of a very fine glacier, cropping out of which were a cluster of remarkable peaks. This glacier rises from a group of mountains, the highest of which attains an altitude of 10,244 feet, and was named by Wheeler, Howser Peak."[4]

Next day, the expedition passed the Falls of Bugaboo Creek and reached the main forks where "a very beautiful view of Harmon's big glacier, which descends right down to the level floor of the valley well amongst timber"[5] met them. Wheeler and Kain climbed through the timber above the forks and established a triangulation station on a bare shoulder of glacial striated rock. Before them a vast panorama unfolded.

At the culminating point of the south fork of Bugaboo Creek was the pass across the Purcell divide which the expedition intended to travel. To the north of the pass was Howser Peak, which they had seen and surveyed the previous day from near the falls. Turning to the northwest looking down on the ice-tongue of Harmon's Glacier, their eyes followed the river of ice up through a tangle of seracs and broken blocks to where the icefield levelled. But there, out of the flatness of the névé, rose the most remarkable nunataks or aiguilles – gray, water streaked, horrendously vertical walls of granite. Conrad Kain found the relief reminiscent of the aiguilles of Chamonix, in France.

They spent a good part of the day on the mountain shoulder photographing and recording Wheeler's surveys, Kain assisting when needed, but mostly gazing at the remarkable aiguilles which rose vertically above the landscape. Certainly, Conrad was enthralled by these granite nunataks. His eye roved the faces and arêtes searching for possible lines of attack. For the moment he could only gaze in rapture, but he would return!

While Kain and Wheeler worked from their vantage point, Harmon and Longstaff explored the snout and surrounding moraines of the glacier a short way up the south fork of Bugaboo Creek. Above the roar of the stream which emanated from beneath the mass of ice, an intermittent cacophony of cracking and crashing was heard. The ice

A.O. Wheeler, T.G. Longstaff, Conrad Kain (behind flames), Charles Lawrence, Bert Barrow and Byron Harmon sitting around evening campfire, 'Longstaff-Wheeler' Bugaboo Expedition, 1910 - Archives of the Canadian Rockies, photo by Byron Harmon

mass, propelled by gravity, worked its way very slowly downstream.

The ice was a very clear blue and the contrast with the dark green of the surrounding forest was beautiful indeed. The lateral moraines, sharply formed, rose high above the glacier. The ice surface was relatively smooth in the lower part, though patterned with cracks and fissures, yielding pleasing lines of blue lacing on an otherwise white landscape.

At a higher level, the half mile wide ice river became a jumble of seracs and ice blocks, falling in two branches on either side of a distinctive nunatak. It featured a remarkably sheer south face and a small patch of snow on its forepeak.[6] To the right of the north fork of the glacier, an immense wall of water-streaked grey granite rose skyward to what seemed a great altitude. It had on the easterly side a small glacier which hung on to who knows what?[7] Beyond was a sharp pointed peak[8] which appeared lower than the others, but because of perspective was thought to be perhaps the highest of the nunataks.

Camp on the forks of the Bugaboo River was highlighted by an interesting and intense discussion of all that had been seen. Enjoying the epi-curean delights of Bert Barrow's culinary talents (grizzly stew), conversation centered on the glacier and its nunataks. Wheeler and Kain related what they had surveyed from up high and Harmon and Longstaff told all they had learned of the glacier. Harmon's glacier was found to be in a phase of retreat with very clean ice and well developed moraines rising on either flank. Longstaff spoke of the peaks shooting up from behind the glaciers "like arctic nunataks out of an icecap: quite sheer, without a speck of snow."[9]

"Ja," replied Conrad in his thick Austrian accent, "dere be no ledges dere to catch dat snow."

Kain realized that here were peaks to challenge the most difficult of all Europe's climbs. Wheeler and Kain talked at length about the peaks they were able to see from the triangulation station and their relative heights. Their interest derived from the fact that the highest peaks[10] were a series of towers rising out of the ice some distance back of the nearest of the nunataks, invisible from the valley of Bugaboo Creek.

On the 10th and 11th days, the weather worsened with snowstorms hitting the party. They managed, however, to reach the crest of the ranges and the watershed between the Bugaboo and Howser Rivers despite the inclement weather. Longstaff investigated the old Bugaboo claim which he refers to as a mine; an outcrop of galena which probably instigated the rush of 1906 in the area.

The expedition to this point was not probing unknown territory. Though perhaps unrecorded, this western slope of the Rocky Mountain Trench had been well explored for mineral resources and soon after the Longstaff-Wheeler expedition, the valleys were invaded for timber resources.

The western slope of the Bugaboo-Howser watershed was something else though. After six days of hard labour and bushwacking, only 12 miles headway was made by the Wheeler-Longstaff party. Because of the prevailing moist Pacific flow of weather, dense foliage flourishes to a greater degree on the western slopes of the Selkirk and Purcell Mountains. The valley bottoms were a nightmarish tangle of slide alder, fallen timber and worst of all, Devil's club.[11]

Trail was made to the north fork of the Howser River by September 18 where the expedition met a trapper. He informed the party that the lower canyon to the Howser River would be impassable for horses. The expedition then divided, Wheeler and Kain returning with the packers and horses to the Columbia via Bugaboo Pass. Longstaff and Harmon proceeded on foot to the Duncan River and the small settlement at Howser Lake. They arrived September 22, 1910.

So began the human involvement and exploration of the Bugaboos. After millions of years of cooling and crystallization of molten rock deep in the earth's crust, uplift and subsequent erosion, years of glaciation and weathering, man finally appeared on the scene. At first the only attractions to the area were economic: mining and trapping. However, the age of mountaineering was dawning upon Canada's cordillera. The challenge was to climb and explore the impossible, and that was the magnetism of the Bugaboos.

Marmolata, Pigeon and Snowpatch Spires tower above Harmon's (Bugaboo) Glacier. 'Longstaff-Wheeler' Bugaboo Expedition 1910. Archives of the Canadian Rockies, photo by Byron Harmon

Marmolata from Boulder Camp - Ed Cooper

Eastpost Creek - J.F. Garden

For six years after the Longstaff-Wheeler expedition of 1910, the nunataks of the Bugaboos saw little or no human activity. In the summer of 1916 two parties of climbers reached the area. The first was that of Dr. Joseph W.A. Hickson and the C.P.R. guide Edward Feuz Jr., who arrived in July. They attempted Howser Peak via the north arête but were turned back by dangerous snow conditions and bad weather.

In August of that summer, a second party organized by Albert H. MacCarthy with the guide Conrad Kain and climbers Henry O. Frind, John and Mrs. Vincent and Mrs. MacCarthy arrived in the area.

During climbs of peaks in the Rockies and Selkirks, MacCarthy had repeatedly seen the far distant Spillimacheen Spires. His curiosity led him to Longstaff's reports in the Geographical Journal and to his guide of many seasons, Conrad Kain, who recounted the sight of the fabulous aiguilles and the country explored during the 1910 expedition.

Albert MacCarthy, from Summit, New Jersey, began his climbing career at the ripe age of 35 in the summer of 1911. His wife Bess was the instigator of MacCarthy's interests as she herself had discovered mountaineering in 1909. From 1911 on, when they purchased the Karmax Ranch on the Columbia River benchland at Wilmer, B.C., the MacCarthy's had spent summers climbing in the Canadian Rockies. In 1913 Conrad Kain and Albert MacCarthy, along with William W. Foster, teamed up to make the first certain ascent of Mt. Robson. From that summer on MacCarthy employed Kain each season as his personal guide and the two became great friends and companions.

Facing page - Snowpatch, Howser and Bugaboo Spires - J.F. Garden

Right - Conrad Kain and Albert McCarthy, 1913 - Archives of the Canadian Rockies, photo by Byron Harmon.

By the year 1916 MacCarthy no doubt had had his ear bent many times with stories of the fabulous aiguilles. So he organized the expedition which he and Kain led into the Bugaboos that season. Their camp, established during mid-August, was about a mile below Harmon's Glacier and provided a good view of the bristling spires of which Kain talked so much and which Longstaff had referred to as "the Nunataks."

The Nunataks, designated as Peaks No. 1, No. 2, and No. 3[1] in Longstaff's articles, were the immediate objectives of this party. At 5 a.m. on the morning of August 26 the expedition marched up the moraine on the north side of Harmon's Glacier, now more often referred to as the Bugaboo Glacier. With Kain leading, the party made their way among the awesome granite spires and ascended toward the col between Peaks 2 and 3[2], reaching it at 9 a.m. Searching for a route up either of the peaks from that natural indentation, the party was very surprised with the view from the col. They gazed out over a far grander vista than any they had yet seen or had imagined existed. Before them, "a broad, more or less circular glacier stretched out and rounded up to rest on the sides of several beautiful spires along its south edge, one of them with its outline capped by an image of a pouter pigeon;[3] at its west side it ran up high on the walls of a lofty ridge that stood in a semi-circle with five sharp peaks vying with each other for leadership,[4] and down in the center of this glacier a long, low ridge showed just above the snow, like a half buried train of cars," wrote MacCarthy.[5]

Discussing all possibilities, looking at all peaks and their possible lines of attack the question arose as to which was the highest. It was hoped that peak No. 3 would be higher than Peak No. 2, as the extreme sheerness of the latter caused it to appear ominous. Peak No. 2 was the most picturesque of all the spires, rising vertically 2,000 feet from the ice, and presenting severe difficulties in the form of overhangs and holdless slabs. Luckily, Peak No. 2 was in fact lower than Peak No. 3. Neither, however, was as lofty as the wall of spires constituting the far western ramparts (Howser Spires) that they gazed upon from the col. The final decision was

to attempt an ascent of the northernmost and highest peak of those ramparts.[6]

Across the glacier towards the train of rocks and the Howser Spires they proceeded. At the west end of the "train of cars," MacCarthy noted the profile of a Sphinx in the rocks, suggesting the name Sphinx Glacier. Kain led his clients through the crevasses on a course which lay up the glacier to the col between the second and third (northernmost) peaks of the Howsers where an enormous bergschrund separated the mountain from the ice.

Above the 'schrund, Kain led the ascent on a 52 degree ice and snow slope to the rocks where a six-inch wide crack was negotiated by jamming sideways with elbows and knees. It was the only route upward, between a vertical slab on the left side and a blank granite wall on the right.

"Three steep snow cornices along the sharp edge of ice ridges then came in rapid succession until we landed in a narrow, horizontal crack at the top of a huge slab that had just begun the descent to its final resting place at the bottom of the valley (where all its companions above were ultimately to join it)," described MacCarthy.[6]

Reaching the high col between the north and middle tower at 2:15 p.m., lunch was enjoyed amidst a spectacularly vertical landscape. The elevation was already higher than the other peaks the party had considered. The east face just ascended was steep though broken, but the west side of the mountain dropped sheer for thousands of feet to a small glacier at the base. This first view of the Howser Towers west face was respectfully noted but not to be climbed until 45 years later.

At 3 p.m. the party continued, described Mac-Carthy ". . .working up the arête, frequently being forced to divert to the east face to avoid smooth boulder sides, and at 10,750 feet our only apparent course carried us through a very small window back of a huge boulder that capped a short rib below. Besides being a tight squeeze for a man and ruck-sack, it had no sill on the opposite side, the footing being a narrow slab edge along the mountain side at right angles to the window, an arrangement that did not commend itself to us as being good architec-

ture. From this point up, there was a series of broken chimneys and a long stretch over uniform water-washed and pitted slopes to a snow cap and a few dry slabs at the summit, to which Mrs. Vincent led us at 4 p.m., our barometer reading 10,950 feet."[7]

With guide Kain protecting, a treacherous but safe descent down a steep ice and snow face off the north ridge was completed. As the afternoon progressed, the 'schrund was crossed to the glacier. The worst was over. MacCarthy's party reached the col between Peaks No. 2 and 3 just as the last rays of after-glow from a brilliant sunset touched the high ramparts of the surrounding spires.

In the valley, all was dark and mostly quiet, except for the clatter of stones as the party descended the glacial moraine and the unceasing roar of water escaping from the glacier below. Overhead in a canopy of brilliant stars the northern lights danced endlessly. By 1 a.m., none of the party could remain awake to enjoy this magnificence of nature. Presumably in their dreams they reflected upon the first ascent of the highest peak of the Howser Spires.

Two days after their successful ascent of the North Howser Spire this intrepid team marched off on a 15 hour traverse of the "Sextet Range." They travelled from the snout of the Bugaboo Glacier up to and over the summit of what is now called Anniversary Peak, then on to the summit of Howser Peak. Returning to the glacier from the mountain a fearsome crevasse had to be crossed. Despite some difficulty, Conrad Kain again led the way with his inventive and cheerful methods of overcoming all difficulties.

In the previous month of July when Dr. J.W.A. Hickson and Ed Feuz had attempted Howser Peak via the north arête, they were turned back by treacherous snow conditions and able to attempt little else in the area. Now in August, MacCarthy and his party were enjoying superb climbing conditions and with the urging of Kain, the ascent of Peak No. 3 was planned.[8]

Howser Towers - J.F. Garden

Mt. Conrad and Bugaboo Spire - J.F. Garden

Albert H. MacCarthy, Mrs. MacCarthy, John Vincent and Conrad Kain left camp at 5:30 a.m. August 29, 1916 and began their approach march to the col between peak No. 2 and Peak No. 3, their sights set on climbing Peak No. 3 via the south ridge which stretches upwards from the col. The weather was initially poor but improved with the day.

For some 1200 feet up the south ridge, the climbing varied with interesting angles and chimneys. Kain and Vincent set a fast pace with Mr. and Mrs. MacCarthy following at a more leisurely gait. At the 10,000 foot level the laggards caught up with Conrad who sat studying a formidable gendarme, "a veritable bugaboo" which suggested "the appropriateness of the name 'Bugaboo' for this spire."[9] The gendarme completely blocked the ridge and the line of ascent. This was the crux of the climb.

To all in the party it appeared that the only route would be up the face of the gendarme. On the left, the mountain fell abruptly to the Sphinx (Vowell) Glacier. To the right was the vertical wall of the east face which descended sheer to a small glacier below. Conrad set to work on the gendarme, ascending some diagonal cracks until he became stuck with no holds, then finally finding the key to the problem, or so MacCarthy thought!

"Half an hour we waited," wrote Albert Mac-Carthy, "while Conrad's body disappeared and reappeared at the edge; after each disappearance we expected to hear a shout that we could prepare to follow, but each time Conrad's fingers would appear again to survey the situation and make a fresh start."[10]

Returning to the base of the gendarme, Conrad decided to tackle the 15 foot perpendicular wall on the left. Using several diagonal cracks as toeholds and friction on the granite, Kain surmounted the first of the gendarme's difficulties.

In Kain's own words: "A few feet higher up was a dent that resembled a saucer from which I studied the surroundings and looked for a way out. It was a tight corner; to my right, the wall I had come up and to the left a holdless slab beyond a short crack, crowned with a slight overhand. Above me a straight wall, 10 or 12 feet, led to a slab, after which nothing was visible except space filled with mist through which a streak of blue ice appeared."

"The only possible way," continued Kain, "was out to the left. There was not room for two on this edge, nor was there a projecting rock or crack for anchorage, so I had to depend entirely on myself. I managed to wriggle over the holdless slab, and when I next tried to get into the crack I was stopped. Convinced that I had started wrong, and as there was no chance to change my position, I crawled back to the edge and began again. To my surprise I found myself in exactly the same position as before; but I grew bolder and stood up, balanced on the toes of my left foot and made great efforts to get into the crack, but could not find a hold."

The Gendarme - J.F. Garden

32

Bugaboo Spire and the Gendarme - James B. Maitre

33

Climbers on the Great Gendarme, Bugaboo Spire - Glen Boles

Above the Gendarme - Roger W. Laurilla

"The endurance required in balancing one's whole weight on the toes should be cultivated," claimed Kain. "Again I returned to the starting point. Searching my memory for something which resembled this bugaboo, I found the picture. Many years ago, in Tyrol, I battled with just such an obstacle as I now had before me. I recollected that I had then overcome it with the aid of an ice-axe; fortunately we had one in the party. My plan was to place the axe in a position to take the weight off the left foot, the only one I could make use of, and at the same time lift myself a few inches higher. This I thought would enable me to put my arm into the crack, which appeared just wide enough so that I could use the elbow on one wall and palm on the other."

"All went well according to this plan," facetiously describes Kain. "Once in the crack the axe was not only useless but proved a real nuisance. I found myself in such a position that I could not dispose of the axe in any other way except by letting it drop. This I would not do, so there was nothing to do but go back once more and make other arrangements."

"Finally, I succeeded in pulling myself up the crack and across the overhang. To my great relief a slanting crack about two inches wide led me to a safe place. I was now only 70 feet above the others, but it had taken me an hour and a half to overcome this stretch."[11]

MacCarthy wrote of Kain's accomplishment: "Just how he finally got into the crack is a mystery to us. But after a dozen reappearances, he smiled and said, 'I make it,' and soon began to call for rope, until about 60 feet had run out and he called from the top of the ridge above the gendarme."[12]

From there, it was up to the first summit at 12:45 where, eyeballing the second peak as being the higher, the party set off for the north summit. The next two hours were spent in reaching that north summit, which according to the barometer was the same as the first, 10,250 feet. After a brief summit respite, descent was made by rappel from the cliffs back of the gendarme down some 80 feet to a small ledge with extreme exposure; 2,000 feet to the snow and ice below. Then the route led back to the ridge below the gendarme and from there an enjoyable scramble down the chimneys and slabs of the south ridge led eventually to the col.

Camp was made by 8 p.m. and a long and very successful day was reflected upon with a new first ascent and a new name for Peak No. 3 – Bugaboo Spire.

CHAPTER THREE:
The Outfitter

The friendship Conrad Kain and Albert Mac-Carthy developed during their many mountain experiences extended beyond the hills they both loved. Kain took up residence at MacCarthy's Karmax Ranch for some years. There, he met Hetta, MacCarthy's maid who became his wife.

Then, in 1920 Kain purchased a small homestead in the area where he operated a guiding and outfitting business during the summer months. He trapped in winter. Kain, with his charm and friendliness, had built up a great number of acquaintances and clients who continued to seek his services year after year.

One of his clients, J. Monroe Thorington, was initially advised by Jimmy Simpson of Banff to hire Kain, and this happenstance was the beginning of a friendship which lasted the remainder of Conrad's life. On a few trips with Thorington, Oliver Eaton Cromwell also came along and in August of 1930 Cromwell engaged Conrad Kain as outfitter and guide to take him into the Bugaboos. Accompanying them were Conrad's wrangler, George Rennenkampf and Cromwell's guide, Peter Kaufmann, from Grindelwald, Switzerland. The party arrived in the Bugaboos on August 5, met by beautiful weather.

On August 6, they made an ascent of Bugaboo Spire via the Kain route; however, Conrad became very ill on that day and could not complete the climb. He was never one to look after his health, seldom protecting himself from the elements or worrying about his own comfort. Cromwell and Kaufmann thoroughly enjoyed the climb and the spectacular vista of the spires. They immediately made plans for the other peaks including Peak No. 2 which, because of an isolated patch of snow halfway up the southeastern face, was christened Snowpatch.

Snowpatch and Pigeon Spires - J.F. Garden

Next day a reconnaissance of Snowpatch Spire was carried out and from all angles it appeared impregnable, the only possible route appeared to be by way of the prominent snowpatch. Conrad Kain himself claimed, "Spire No. 2, with sheer cliffs on all sides, is the most picturesque of all and rises some 2,000 feet above the glacier. After carefully searching with powerful binoculars I came to the conclusion that this pinnacle will prove very hard to conquer. Since, I have had the opportunity to study the peak from different angles, and have not changed my opinion. I feel inclined to prophesy that this pinnacle will be the most difficult ascent in the Canadian Alps."[1]

Snowpatch Spire seemed hopeless but Pigeon (Peak No. 1) remained unclimbed – and its western ridge looked quite feasible for a first ascent. Setting off from Bugaboo – Snowpatch col, the long western ridge was reached after a lengthy tramp across the glacier and was followed easily as far as the first minor summit.

"The aspect of the ridge from there, which leads up to the shoulder was so formidable," Cromwell writes, "that we seriously considered a retreat. However, one cannot tell by looking."[2]

Soon he and Kaufmann found themselves on a shoulder, separated from the summit proper by a deep notch. The summit itself seemed impossible. Traversing around the difficulties, a chimney was discovered which led upwards on the northwest face.

"Sloping ledges brought us around to the north ridge," Cromwell relates, "which we gained by an interesting jamcrack just large enough to permit the insertion of right fist and knee. This led away at an angle of approximately 45 degrees, and after 30 or 40 feet petered out into a 'finger traverse', the key of the climb. While I belayed the rope as securely as I could, Peter crept carefully along, supported as much by the friction of his clothes against the rock as by the narrow crevice into which he slipped his fingers. The ridge once gained, 10 minutes of easy going brought us to the left summit and a magnificent panorama of the group."[3]

Descent was accomplished along the western ridge, then down the south side onto the Bugaboo Glacier. Navigating down a long windridge of snow among crevasses, the great southeast slabs of Pigeon Spire and the vertical south wall of Snowpatch Spire rose overhead. The impressiveness of Snowpatch was emphasized from this angle and supported Kain's opinion of the impregnability of this mountain. But Pigeon was now climbed and appropriate celebration was made of that when Cromwell and Kaufmann arrived in camp at 7 p.m. to the greetings and congratulations of Kain and Rennenkampf.

Pigeon Spire, west ridge - Roger W. Laurilla

Bugaboo and Snowpatch from the summit of Pigeon Spire - Rob Rohn

The party lingered in the area for three more days as the weather held. On August 8, Cromwell and Kaufmann climbed the Howser Spires via Kain and MacCarthy's route of 1916. On August 10, they decided to celebrate Conrad Kain's birthday by attempting Center Peak, also known as Marmolata. Kain was now feeling healthy again and so accompanied Cromwell and Kaufmann.

Across from Snowpatch, over the glacier above the icefall, they proceeded to the saddle in the north ridge of Center Peak; the ridge led straight to the top with excellent and interesting climbing, in places of a high degree of difficulty.

Pigeon Spire viewed from the north with the west ridge profiled on the right - J.F. Garden

Cromwell wrote of this adventure; "Just below the summit, we were stopped by a vertical, holdless pitch some 12 to 15 feet in height. This Conrad beat by taking a back-stand furnished by Peter and myself, inserting the pick of his ice-axe into a horizontal fissure, and swarming up the handle until he could get his fingers into the crack. From there he swung out to the right, found a small ledge, and was up. I didn't find it very easy, being the last. The axe came away, and I was left suspended like Mahomet's coffin, twixt heaven and earth, until a long pull, brought me also to the top. We had used some three hours on the ridge; and it was now 5 o'clock."[4]

Descending via the same route, camp was made at 9 p.m., though it had been planned to return down the south ridge had time not been short.

Finally on August 11, a traverse was made of the two little peaks at the head of the main Bugaboo Glacier, Thimble and Flat Top. The excursion was devoid of any climbing difficulties, but they witnessed a sensational view of the western wall and South Tower of the Howsers. That hidden and perhaps most spectacular wall of the Bugaboos remained unclimbed until 1961 and was certainly as "impossible" as Snowpatch in 1930.

Yet to come were new methods and equipment in the art of mountain climbing, and much controversy as to the merits and fairness of the use of artificial climbing aids in overcoming such difficulties as were to be found on Snowpatch and the west faces of the Howser Spires.

Anniversary Peak and Marmolata at sunrise - J.F. Garden

Mt. Conrad - Dan Graydon

Conrad Kain and J. Monroe Thorington on Trapper Peak (later named Mt. Conrad), July 1933. Archives of the Canadian Rockies

Early in 1933, Conrad's wife, Hetta, died. It was a great blow to Conrad and he found himself very lonely and depressed. In correspondence, J. Monroe Thorington related that he would be coming west that summer. Kain hopefully wrote, "If you find someone to join you I will give you my possible lowest rates. If you have to come alone, and I have nothing on hand I take you up the Bugaboo for $5 (five dollar) per day, I supply the grub and climb with you, you wash the dishes."[5]

In June of that year Thorington was finally able to make a trip into the Bugaboos with Conrad Kain. No doubt Kain had told him enthusiastically all about his favourite aiguilles, but until this late date Thorington had never seen the granite spires which so obsessed Conrad. Though it was very early in the season for climbing anything in the Bugaboos, the first recorded ascent of Crescent Spires was accomplished.

In the American Alpine Journal, J. Monroe Thorington wrote of this trip into the Bugaboos with Conrad Kain:

"Conrad and I made an ascent into the northeast corner of the group on June 27, following a goat trail from the middle of the north lateral moraine into a snow basin where there are two small frozen lakes. Without great difficulty we were the first to stand upon the summit just northeast of Bugaboo Spire; it is about 9,400 feet high with two large gendarmes on its south ridge. Its position and shape suggest the name of Crescent Spire and, as a viewpoint, it is magnificent."[6]

The trip with Thorington was chiefly for topographical work, Thorington generally surveying and investigating the area. It would be the last trip these two good friends shared. That summer Kain climbed Mt. Louis again (on his 50th birthday) and visited the ACC camp in Paradise Valley where he met Professor and Mrs. Igor A. Richards. With them he returned to the Bugaboos where they climbed Pigeon Spire and later the highest peak of the Bobbie Burns group which at that time was unnamed, but has since been entitled Mt. Conrad. It was his last climb.

Conrad Kain died on February 2, 1934. He was a great story teller, companion and guide. Though he often doubted his own accomplishments and purpose in life, he greatly influenced the world of alpinism, advancing the art of climbing and bringing much respect to the guiding community. In Canada his name has become legend.

The Bugaboos are as much a part of Conrad Kain as he was a part of them. A mountain hut built high above the Bugaboo Glacier, within the shadows of Snowpatch Spire has been named in Kain's honour. The Bugaboo Recreation Area, set aside and administered by the Province of British Columbia preserves the legacy of a great mountaineer and the peaks he loved.

Gone is the man, but a legend remains, entwined in the history of Canada's mountains and in particular, the Bugaboos.

Right - Crescent Spire - J.F. Garden

Below - Mt. Conrad - Roger W. Laurilla

Facing page - Profile of the west buttress, Howser Towers - Scott Flavelle.

Ralph Bennetsen rappelling the Kraus-McCarthy route on
Snowpatch Spire - Roger W. Laurilla

PART II:
THE HARD MEN

Climbers working the east face of Snowpatch Spire - James B. Maitre

During the period of the first explorations and climbs in the Bugaboos (1910-1935), skills and techniques utilized in climbing in North America remained relatively unchanged. Protection from a fall was basically dependent on the strength of the belayer, and in fact, belaying was not much more than hanging on to the rope with one's hands.

From the beginnings of the sport of mountain climbing, devices of one sort or another have always been utilized to enable a climber to ascend. The ice-axe, or alpen-stock was a combination walking stick and ice-pick. The rope was of Manila or Italian hemp, unelastic, largely untested and of less than half the strength of modern nylon. Pitons and their use as protection while climbing were as yet unheard of in North America, and to use them as a means of scaling a peak was a serious question of morals! Direct aid of any kind was considered ungentlemanly in conservative circles of the climbing fraternity and to climb in such an unsporting manner was very much a serious breach of ethics.

During the early years of the 20th Century, however, the use of iron pegs began in the Eastern Alps of Europe. At first used only in belay protection, this development was to lead inevitably to the use of aid in overcoming the very difficult climbing problems of the future. By this time in Europe everything of importance had been climbed, so the attention of ambitious climbers became focused on the great walls and other various route possibilities unscaled. In North America it was not until perhaps 1940 that such a refocusing of ambitions came about. Up until then there were endless new ascents to be completed.

At first, the big wall climbs of Bavaria and Tyrol, and the Dolomites were free. In 1908, the first recorded Grade V route was ascended on the South West Face of the Campanile Basso in the Dolomites by Rudolph Fehrmann and Oliver Perry-Smith. A gymnast from Munich, Anton Schmid was also pushing Grade V and better in Bavaria and the Tyrol. Italian climbers Tita Piaz and Angelo Dibona were far ahead of contemporaries in their home mountains, the Dolomites. Piaz in 1911 completed a short but strenuous Grade VI free climb on Torre Winkler, North East Face. Dibona in 1910 climbed the South West Face of Croz dell'Altissimo at V+ and though he was at the time experimenting with peg and rope manoeuvres, he and Luigi Rizzi climbed that thousand metre face entirely free.

The extension of artificial aids in Europe began after 1910 when crampons were first introduced. The evolution of the karabiner, closely associated with the names Otto Herzog and Hans Fiechtl, and the subsequent use of it in conjunction with pitons led to experimentation with the use of double rope methods in direct aid. Hans Dülfer was the pioneer of these methods and is said to be the inventor of such manuevers as the modern rappel, the pendulum, and friction traverses. Dülfer, it is said, was the 'true forgoer of the Grade 6'.[1]

Dülfer had a friend at the time, who believed in climbing free. His name was Paul Preuss, also from Munich, and as well as being a leading contender of free climbing, was also one of the earliest of the solo climbers in alpine history. Unfortunately he met his demise on a solo climb in 1913, but Dülfer's fate was far crueler – he died in an artillery barrage in 1915 during the First World War!

One climber who also figured in the development of aid climbing was Fritz Wiessner, a German who made his reputation in the Eastern Alps before emigrating to North America. His emigration seems to have coincided with the birth of aid climbing in North America. Prior to the middle 1930's wall climbing was not in practise and areas such as Yosemite had never seen much of roped climbing, let alone direct aid on its massive granite walls. However, when such methods were introduced, their use certainly wasn't spared.

John Salathé, a native of Switzerland, was perhaps the great instigator of aid climbing in North America. His ascent of the South West Face of Half Dome in 1946 with Anton Nelson, using his self-forged Salathé pitons, destroyed the infamous reputation of this wall. They made the ascent in twenty-one hours and avoided the use of bolts which had become popular on such climbs as

Roger Laurilla on the summit of Snowpatch Spire, the Howser Towers and Pigeon Spire in the background - Roger W. Laurilla

Shiprock in 1939. Revolutionizing the design and material of pitons, Salathé began the impressive American development of climbing equipment and paraphernalia, much of which was re-introduced to Europe in the 1960's by Royal Robbins, John Harlin and Gary Hemmings.

As in Europe a new breed of climber was to emerge upon the rock faces of North America. The "hard" climbers or so-called "hard men" were dedicated to defeating the challenge of unclimbed walls and faces, no matter whether on mountains or local quarries. Free from the traditional bonds and conservative restraints of long established organizations, Americans began a method of climbing that seemed from the start to be extreme aid (bolts) and to later advance to more refined and esthetic methods with the development of more modern equipment. It seemed at first, to the chagrin of the established climbing world, that these men knew no restrictions and were game to try any available method to achieve their ambitions. As a result, climbing in North America almost seems to have begun from where Europeans left off prior to World War II and has since evolved far more rapidly than elsewhere.

On the walls and pinnacles of the United States, mostly in Yosemite Valley, the hard men honed their skills, training themselves and developing the new techniques required for the "big walls" of North America. Advances in the design of pitons and

bolts, nylon ropes and other gear raced ahead as climbers turned inventors. The idea of multi-day climbs involving bivouacs on a mountain face became practicable with the advent of new equipment and clothing. Stronger and lighter materials, and their application in the design and use of innovative equipment such as the aluminum carabiner made wall climbing far more feasible.

Not only were more outlandish climbs achieved with the new developments, but the safety aspect advanced. Body belays, friction belays, piton belays, all became standard procedure. The use of pre-tested and stronger nylon ropes, body harnesses and nylon webbing, and hard hats, led to greater individual protection. Big wall climbing developed as a true sport, rather than a dare-devil exhibition or death-defying stunt which many people previously thought it to be. The risks were being minimized. The sport was becoming a less hazardous proposition.

But were the risks really lessened? It has been pointed out that the risks in climbing have proceeded upward with the development of new equipment that allows the climber to push the "limits." For instance tiny pitons and chocks have made possible some extreme wall climbs, but now the climber is on a big wall rather than a less technical, less risky climb. Whatever the risks, the sport has definitely taken on new directions with the advent of modern technology and techniques.

Snowpatch Spire, the last unclimbed mountain of the Bugaboo group proved to be a most difficult problem indeed, just as Conrad Kain had prophesied. Its sheerness on all sides made the route possibilities discouraging. Only on the southeast quadrant of the mountain was there anything but characteristically sheer, often overhanging walls. On that side closest to Bugaboo Glacier, the lower part of the mountain is more broken into large granitic blocks. The mountain then sweeps upwards from the large snowpatch, from which its name is derived, to the 10,050 foot South Summit.

In July of 1938 a party of Americans led by Fritz Wiessner arrived in the Bugaboos with hopes of attempting and completing the first ascent of Snowpatch Spire. Included in the expedition were two ladies, Marguerite Schnellbacher and Polly Prescott as well as Messrs. Laurence Coveney, Chappell Cranmer and Sterling B. Hendricks. Though logging roads were beginning to encroach on the furthest recesses of the Purcell Mountains and access was becoming easier year by year, approaching the area was still a major expeditionary undertaking. The services of an experienced outfitter and weeks of time were still required to penetrate the 25 miles from the Columbia River to the Bugaboos.

During this expedition a first ascent of Brenta Spire was recorded and on July 12 a majority of the group climbed the North Howser Spire, marking the third ascent of that mountain. While North Howser was being climbed Wiessner and Coveney split from the party and attempted the unclimbed South Tower of the Howser Spires. This was the first known attempt on the sharp southernmost Spire of the Howser massif. However, they were halted near the centre of the spire as all efforts to scale an ice-filled chimney and the rock which surrounded it proved fruitless. Perhaps it was still too early in the season for such an accomplishment.[1]

Snowpatch from Crescent Spire - Glen Boles

On July 14, Wiessner and Cranmer decided to have a go at Snowpatch Spire, beginning their ascent from the col on the south-east shoulder below the mountain's prominent snowpatch. The climbing proved every bit as difficult as forecast. Their route followed a series of cracks upward to a sharp-edged ridge. Above the ridge the first overhanging zone was encountered and somewhere above that lay the prominent snowpatch.

Once at the first overhanging zone the real difficulties began and so too the artificial climbing! Wiessner forced his way over the overhangs using six pitons and rope slings in aid. The time required for this strenuous effort was considerable however, consuming so much of their day that when easy slabs leading to the snowpatch were finally reached, daylight was waning. Their view of the upper face of the mountain was discouraging, their route appeared to present even more formidable difficulties than they had yet encountered. Short of pitons and short of daylight, they withdrew from the mountain.

It was a valiant effort; the first attempt not only of Snowpatch Spire but of overcoming extreme climbing in the Bugaboos with the use of aid. Wiessner's attempt foreshadowed events to happen in the coming decades of climbing in the Bugaboos. Now it would be left to others to prove the pragmatists wrong about Snowpatch.

During the summer of 1940, Jack Arnold, Fritz Lippman, Edward Koskinen and Raffi Bedayn arrived in the Bugaboos bent on proving that Snowpatch was not as invincible as claimed.

"Sitting under a fiery August sun," Bedayn wrote, "we were contemplating another attack on the bugaboo of the Bugaboos, Snowpatch Spire. Beginning with Conrad Kain and culminating in the gallant attempt of Fritz Wiessner, nine attempts over a period of 24 years had put Snowpatch on the 'unclimbable' class."[2]

Beginning on August 2, Koskinen and Lippman on a reconnaissance, climbed from the notch to the snowpatch on the mountain. It was their opinion that the route that Wiessner pioneered would not go. However, Jack Arnold and Raffi Bedayn were

of the opinion that it was the only feasible route. They made their preparations and gathered equipment for a possible bivouac on the mountain. Pitons, carabiners, hammers, ropes and slings, as well as a (Zeltsack) bivy bag were assembled and the decision made to try to push a route above the snowpatch up past Wiessner's high point.

From Snowpatch notch on August 4, Arnold and Bedayn, using crepe shoes, worked their way over Wiessner's overhang and on up high angle friction slabs to the base of the snowpatch. The upper face appeared awesome, nothing but overhangs! It looked as if the mountain would be more of an engineering project than a climb. The environment they found themselves in was a cold and stark granite desert, pitched at right angles. "In our extremely difficult climbing in Yosemite Valley," Bedayn writes, "we learned to appreciate the trees that pushed themselves up here and there on sheer faces. They were one of the best friends a climber could want. Here we had none."[3]

Such was the difference between the high angle walls on which Americans developed their aid climbing skills, and the big walls of the Bugaboos. They had transferred their skills from relatively sheltered though technically difficult valley walls to wide open alpine peaks, complete with all the objective dangers that nature could put forth in a high mountain environment. Not only were there vertical walls and overhangs but ice and snow, rain and wind, thunder and lightning. Good weather was something the Bugaboos were not well known for. Standing high and isolated in their surroundings, the Spires are susceptible to all the weather that blows eastward from the Pacific Ocean.

On Snowpatch the rule found cold hands and feet soaked in water-drenched couloirs, cracks where ice lingered from the previous winter; slippery moss covering hand and foot holds and wide granite slabs great for friction but with such roughness that skin was torn off hands and knees.

Adequate belay positions were hard to find. Pitons, anchors and double rope techniques were definitely required. Needless to say, Bedayn and Arnold did not advance too far above the snowpatch that first day and so they spent a night on the moun-

tain, descending to the notch where they had started but only after downclimbing the Wiessner overhang in semi-darkness.

"Two hours after dawn we were putting the finishing touches on a modicum of cheese and chocolate. We noticed our food bag had been broken into during the night, a large hole in one corner giving ample evidence. Checking to see what was gone, we missed the tablets brought along to furnish the necessary vitamins absent in the concentrated food. Further investigation indicated that a 'snafflehound' had done this to us."[4]

Bedayn was describing another "objective danger" that the Bugaboo environment presents to climbers. Snafflehounds, the guilty rodents Bedayn discusses, are bushy tailed wood-rats or pack-rats which exist in the mountain environs of western North America. Unsuspecting climbers are invariably set upon by these rodents whose tastes range from slings to boots, packs and human food. Especially populous in the Bugaboos, pack-rats are an undeniably hazardous threat to climbers, especially as they have developed an epicurean taste for new, unused nylon rope!

Bedayn and Arnold returned to the high point of the previous day's climb. For many hours they worked the overhangs above the snowpatch but they were unable to get anywhere. Then on looking around Bedayn discovered a small ledge which led towards the middle of the spire, directly above the snowfield a thousand feet below. Through two short chimneys they jammed upwards then Bedayn led a zig-zag route around an overhanging nose to an apparent deadend on a sloping shelf overshadowed by yet another overhang.

This offered no hope as various attempts to surmount the overhang were tried. The only way, and the crux of the entire climb, seemed to rest in getting up a near vertical dike of broken aplite

Ralph Bennetsen climbing the Wiessner overhang on Snowpatch Spire - Roger W. Laurilla

which extended up to the base of an overhang some 20 feet above. The line itself was stepped, but handholds and footholds on the wall other than the dike itself were non-existent. Bedayn placed pitons in the aplite, but ran out halfway up and had to descend for more.[5]

"Back up I climbed to the highest piton," relates Bedayn, "inserted another to protect my advance, then looked desperately for a bucket handhold, which didn't exist. There was, however, a small patch of some minute plant about a foot higher than I could reach from my present stance. Moving up a little on the vein I was able to dig out this small depression, large enough to maintain a balance with two fingers, a linger-but-don't-stop handhold. Suddenly on my left I caught sight of a moving object, a small brown animal, scampering on the friction pitch that I had given up. To my chagrin I recognized the critter. It was undoubtably the snafflehound romping around full of our vitamins. I needed them now."[6]

"Soon I was able to hammer in another piton. Three steps brought me underneath the overhang. A scree-covered mantel-shelf large enough to permit a finger traverse continued on a horizontal plane. Driving in a bomb-proof piton, I began traversing. There wasn't much to rest the feet on while doing this little piece, and it seemed best to do it quickly."[7]

Jack Arnold found this a very difficult traverse indeed, using his right forearm and fingers to inch his way across.

"Eight feet and a few seconds later," continued Bedayn, "I was circumnavigating a huge chockstone at the edge of this traverse and the lichen covered granite slab. Standing on the chockstone I gave vent to my feelings, a hoarse yodel. Arnold came up a few minutes later to see what was wrong."[8] From that point on the mountain, it was up a small high-angle gully, a traverse right, and up with quite a bit of difficulty through a chimney blocked by two chockstones.

"Above was a three inch crack with a blank left wall, and a right side that didn't possess anything which might be termed useful, it simply dropped

Moss Campion on Snowpatch Spire - J.F. Garden

off to the glacier below. Twelve feet of this three inch crack and I was able to stand on a foot square pedestal."[9]

Arnold came on up and somehow the two climbers managed to stand crowded on the foot square area. Continuing on up the crack, it ended in yet another overhang with no apparent way beyond. Once there however, the wall on the left opened up out to the main face. Up came Arnold to that stance where again he belayed as Bedayn climbed upward.

"Things were looking a great deal better. Proceeding once more I noticed a pencil of light on the loose granite blocks, and crossed over to check its source. I was amazed when I saw the summit, and so was Jack, who came up quickly. We hadn't expected the summit so soon."[10] After 23 pitons – two used in direct aid – Bedayn and Arnold found themselves the first men to have climbed Snowpatch Spire.

After celebrating their easier than expected success, a descent of four long rappels interspersed with sections of downclimbing put them back at the notch in three hours. Collecting gear left there, it was discovered that a snafflehound had lunched on their leather boot tops and tongues. No doubt, the heritage of packrats in general was severely questioned!

CHAPTER FIVE:
The Last Bugaboo

By August of 1941 all the major peaks of the Bugaboos had been climbed except the Central and South towers of the Howser Spires.

The South Howser Tower stands vertically isolated from the less spectacular Central and North Towers. On all sides it is extremely steep with only the eastern side allowing for any obvious routes of ascent. Attracted by this virgin peak, four members of the Seattle Mountaineers, Lloyd Anderson, Lyman Boyer, Tom Campbell and Helmy Beckey, arrived in the Bugaboos, intent on completing this first ascent.

At 4:00 a.m. on Tuesday, August 5, the four climbers set off over the Vowell Glacier towards a previously scouted route up the east face of the mountain. The difficulties began immediately as a bergschrund on the steep lower ice slopes separated the entire South Tower from the Vowell Glacier.

Standing on the lower lip of the crevasse, the party eyed the 10 foot ice wall which hung three feet out over them. Beginning where the 'schrund drops away to the left, an attempt was made to traverse from the lower lip over to the upper lip. At that point it is not so much higher. Boyer worked his way across, actually inside the choked bergschrund and with some difficulty, finding solid ice, cut his way through the overhang. Once on the upper lip, he brought the others across to where a 60 degree ice-slope led upward to the outcropping rocks left of the main ice couloir. "At least no one has been this far," Boyer remembers someone saying.[1]

Step-cutting up the snow covered ice-slope, after four hours, Boyer finally reached the smooth granite slabs of the South Tower. The only likely route appeared up an 80 foot chimney of mixed rock and ice, topped off by a chockstone among loose rubble. That obstacle required stemming and a strenous pull-up and as a result much loose rock

South Howser Tower from the east. The route first climbed led upward near the long snowslope on the left of the face then out into the centre of the face around the small prominent snowpatch and upward to the final summit - J.F. Garden

would come rattling down the chimney. Despite care and caution Boyer received a stunning blow from one fusillade, a bloody gash required first aid assistance before the party could venture further.

During the advancing afternoon, the climbers negotiated a broken granite face of near 50 degree steepness on mixed snow and rock, and a steep ice couloir topped by a mound of ice. On the rock of the shoulder at the head of the main ice couloir on the south face, a bivouac was established at 7:00 p.m. They were halfway up.

"Into this sheltered refrigerator we huddled," wrote Lloyd Anderson. "Between shifts during the night we discovered we had a crag rat stealing what was left of our food supply."[2] The now infamous snafflehounds of the Bugaboo Spires, though probably surprised by this strange and unprecedented appearance of life, wasted no time in taking advantage of the occasion.

The following morning an attempt was made to place a route directly up the ridge above the bivouac. After four hours this proved to be a fruitless effort. On Beckey's suggestion Lloyd Anderson led out along a ledge onto the northeast face. Circling around the lower part of the snowpatch he reached a steep, rock jammed and ice filled couloir which appeared as if it would lead somewhere. Boyer pushed upward through the couloir to a 25 foot vertical jam crack on an exposed face. On the left was a horizontal slot in the wall, large enough to jam in a leg for security in belaying the remainder of the party. Working up the sloping rock above that crack, a deep indentation of the ridge was reached only 150 vertical feet above the previous night's bivouac!

"Ahead was a pitch which seemed impossible," wrote Boyer. "On either side, the face dropped sheer. A 40 foot wall ended in a slightly overhanging pitch of 10 feet. A heavy growth of lichen added difficulty. However, a 15 foot pinnacle in front of the wall offered a possible start. Lloyd (Anderson) mounted the pinnacle, placed two pitons as high as he could reach, and prepared to belay Lyman (Boyer). The latter climbed the pinnacle, (then) stepped over Lloyd (Anderson) onto the wall. Mov-

ing rapidly up to the overhang, he drove in a piton and anchored. Using direct aid technique, he raised himself four feet and reached a handhold above the overhang, but the rope jammed in the carabiner and it was only with the greatest difficulty that he swung himself up to the ledge above."[3]

Only 100 feet to the summit! Getting there meant conquering a steep, exposed ridge with parallel vertical cracks giving good handholds, then a broad ridge, followed by the summit. At 4:00 p.m. Lloyd Anderson in the lead stood aside to allow Lyman Boyer the honour of being first on the summit.

"Helmy, the youngest of the group informed us that it was his birthday, his sixteenth," Boyer noted.[4] It was Helmy's older brother, Fred, who would dominate the future events which were to take place during the coming years in the Bugaboos.

Because of the attitude of British and Canadian Alpine Clubs and their reluctance to consider the validity of technical aid climbing, few climbers other than Americans ventured into the Bugaboos. The establishment climbers remained adamant on the scandalous use of pitons and other aid devices. After having done so much to open up the Canadian alpine scene, to have explored and climbed so many inaccessible areas, to have achieved great strides in the promotion of alpinism, these people refused to accept the new ideas which were to expand the limits of the sport.

Big wall climbers, often referred to as hard men, developed new and technically advanced standards of climbing during the late 30's and into the 40's. Experimenting on the vertical walls of relatively protected areas such as Yosemite, great strides were made in extending the horizons of rock climbing.

With the standards being pushed as they were, it was only a matter of time before the skills learned in Yosemite were applied to the walls of the high alpine peaks. As photographs and word of imposing vertical spires in British Columbia circulated throughout the climbing world, it became apparent that a great challenge lay in conquering the granite walls which existed in the Bugaboos.

South Howser Tower from Pigeon Spire - J.F. Garden

Howser Towers - James B. Maitre

Pigeon Spire with the north couloir climbed by Beckey, Heib and Widrig clearly visible in the centre of the photo - J.F. Garden

CHAPTER SIX:
Fred Beckey Arrives

Foremost among the new breed of American climbers to discover the Bugaboos and their immense walls was Fred Beckey. A native of Germany, Fred along with his brother Helmy resided in Seattle, an ideal location considering the proximity of the North Cascades.

Starting in their middle teens, the two brothers spent a great deal of time experimenting with new techniques and climbing skills, once working out on a face cushioned at the base with snow, should anything go wrong. The Cascades provided them with a vast playground to hone their skills and test their physical stamina, and in those mountains they achieved a number of first ascents.

By the summer of 1942, Fred and Helmy were excellent mountaineers, and a strong climbing team. Still in their teens, they decided that July to tackle Mt. Waddington in British Columbia's Coast Range. Their trip was a great success – they achieved the second ascent of this remote giant.

Old-line mountaineers were dumbfounded at the uninhibited ambitions and skills of the Beckey boys and the climbing world was awed when they completed that second ascent of Waddington, a peak of over 13,000 feet which had seen 16 attempts end in failure, before its first ascent in 1936.

During the war years, Beckey served in the U.S. Army Mountain Troops and following the war he made his first climbs in the Yosemite Valley and joined an expedition to Alaska which successfully made first ascents of Kates Needle and the Devils Thumb. These were very difficult technical climbs in a severe climate, though both peaks were ascended on fine days. Fred Beckey was becoming a noted alpinist of great skill and determination. In 1947 he returned to the Waddington area where, with the Harvard Mountaineering Club, he made nine first ascents during a two-month stay. Then in July of 1948 he travelled to Banff, in the Canadian Rockies, where he made an ascent of Mount Louis; then went over to the Columbia Valley and up the logging roads of Bugaboo Creek.

In the Bugaboos, Fred Beckey was to achieve pioneering ascents during the next 15 years. Arriving at Boulder Camp above the Bugaboo Glacier,

directly under the eastern walls of Snowpatch and Bugaboo Spires, Beckey and his friends Ralph Widrig and Joe Hieb gazed at what many considered the greatest technical problems of the time. During the next few days, they climbed. On the classic Kain route of Bugaboo Spire, Beckey had to admire the capabilities of the legendary guide. The gendarme pitch is still a difficult move today and in Conrad Kain's day climbers wore nailed boots and had little protection against a fall.

On July 17, Widrig, Hieb and Beckey placed a new route up the 1,500 foot north face of Pigeon Spire. Their way to the base of the mountain went up the Warren icefall between Snowpatch and Pigeon. Hacking steps up broken ice ridges they came to the bergschrund which separates ice from rock. Across the abyss was the north couloir where their planned route to the summit lay.

"A great rock couloir," Beckey wrote, "well adorned with verglas, split the cliffs west of the little

Jim Maitre ascending the Gendarme on Bugaboo Spire - J.F. Garden

pinnacle low on the north arête, leading to a large ice patch. Above that, the face promised no continuous route, but we decided to try anyhow, feeling the challenge of exploratory climbing."[1]

Crossing the bergschrund the climb proceeded up a 50 degree ice pitch, then up a grey couloir; vertical walls with an ice coated overhang topping it off. Hieb took over the lead, traversing a vertical rib on a fingertip ledge, then back into the couloir negotiating another overhang.

The next lead was unbelievably difficult. Hieb jammed his way up narrow vertical cracks, driving a piton while hanging on to next to nothing. He was able to advance up a smooth face on the left to an overhang which was overcome with the aid of pitons for tension. A slanted, snowy ledge provided a belay station where Widrig took over.

Unable to climb the dry right side of the couloir, Widrig, with a semi-tension belay ". . .traversed left to an awkward corner," wrote Beckey, "and somehow found a high clutch hold that enabled him to squirm breathlessly onto a minute ledge beneath the iced, dripping overhang. . ."[2] that they had observed from below. Resigning himself to climbing the overhang direct or not at all, Widrig was able to place an angle piton high above him as water gushed down his arm. Standing in a sling, groping around for a handhold, he found that the rock was totally coated with verglas. So he started chipping away the ice and it came whizzing down the couloir dangerously threatening Hieb and Beckey below.

"Widrig worked up to a point where he placed an angle piton, inserted a sling, and repeated the process," writes Beckey. "Dangling high over the void, he worked some time with the hammer to remove loose snow and ice on the wall above. Finally, he uncovered a side-cling hold for his left hand, after almost giving up because of the absence of either holds or cracks. Pulling himself to an awkwardly balanced position, he quickly pounded a piton, carried between his teeth, and leaning far to the right, made a tension traverse around a glazed, bulging overhang to reach a belay ledge with one foot of the 120 foot nylon to spare."[3]

He shouted that everything looked better above; the others came up and Hieb took over the lead again. "After muscling up a vertical flake," wrote Beckey, "he wormed up a very difficult wall that at once bulged into an overhang."[4] This was the extreme of fifth class climbing, Hieb making his way up a series of grooved, nearly impossible cracks, the rope dangling vertically behind him. The big ice patch was finally reached, every pitch having required delicate balance as well as extreme muscular tension.

Beckey led for some distance, hacking up ice, then working a series of ledges onto the north arête above the ice patch. The ascent was now reaching the final effort.

Only one route appeared feasible above, a long 140 foot slab, angling off at 70 degrees and cleft by a deep two foot crack. Hieb commanded this very touchy and exposed lead using laybacks and stemming by muscular contraction and expansion. Halfway up the long crack Hieb belayed Widrig up, who then gave a shoulder to get Hieb up a holdless 10 foot step beyond the crack. Even this move "called for perfect balance and pressure climbing," wrote Beckey.[5]

"Joyous yells announced that it was a 'sure thing' now," recalled Beckey, "for the remaining route to the summit was in full view."[6] Two more leads of ice cutting, and a mad scramble was made for the summit, reached at 7 p.m. after over seven hours on the face.

Lingering on the summit they reflected on their climb and the sights of the surrounding spires. Beckey describes the scene and his thoughts:

"Evening shadows deepened the tones of the valleys. A reddish alpine glow illuminated the sky beyond Howser and its terrific South Tower. We looked with interest at the west walls of Snowpatch and Bugaboo. Behind the Bobbie Burns group, we spied Sir Donald, and in other directions we saw the Goodsirs, Ethelbert and the line of the high Purcell summits to the south. Though prejudiced perhaps by their nearness, I felt that the Bugaboos were the most spectacular peaks I had seen in Canada outside of the Coast Range."[7]

Descending into darkness, they made their way down the west ridge of Pigeon, then across the Vowell Glacier to the Bugaboo-Snowpatch col. Hoots and hollers echoed through the darkened spires as they made exhilarating glissades down from the col on the steep and long snowslopes leading back to Boulder Camp.

Before departing the Bugaboos, Hieb, Widrig and Beckey made further ascents. On July 20th they climbed Snowpatch by the Wiessner overhang in just over five hours. On July 21 the group climbed the Crescent by new routes on six of its spires. This trip marked the beginning of a preference for and a mastery of steep faces which Beckey was to pursue with great ambition and success.

Beckey had his sights set on climbing the supposedly impossible walls of the Bugaboo Spires.

Though Beckey, Hieb and Widrig enjoyed success in their climbs of 1948, that summer marked a tragic accident in the Bugaboos. When one speaks of the "objective dangers" of alpine climbing, it is generally a reference to acts of nature which no individual can control. One of the most serious

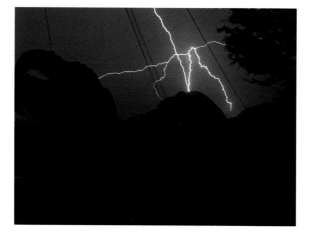

As seen through the maze of wires and radio antenna from the back porch of the Conrad Kain Hut, lightning strikes the summit of Bugaboo Spire - Jim Weston

objective dangers in climbing is the weather, and lightning storms are the most dangerous of storms. Stories abound in climbing lore relating incidents of lightning strikes.

The story of such an event is tragic. A climbing party comprised of Rolf Pundt, Robert Becker, Cricket Strong and Ian MacKinlay were climbing Bugaboo Spire and had arrived above the great gendarme when a violent thunderstorm overtook them.

From Ian MacKinlay's account:

"Bob was all for going on to the further summit, but by the time we got started the static charge had built up to such a degree that all the points in the vicinity were emitting sparks and the air was filled with a violent hissing."[8]

Shelter was taken in a cave formed by a large block of granite, some 100 feet below the summit. Ian continued:

"We had the rucksacks open and were about to have lunch when the next thing that I recall was that I was flat on my back, paralyzed from the neck down. I could see Rolf staggering outside the cave and I yelled at him to stop. He gave one great lurch and went over the side."[9]

Bob was unconscious. Ian MacKinlay and Cricket Strong rappelled down the mountain with great difficulty as they were badly burned. They hurried as best they could to get help for Bob. Cricket fell some 250 feet down the lower scree slopes ending in the avalanche debris of the Bugaboo-Snowpatch col.

Attempts to return and get the unconscious Bob Becker were impossible as a ferocious snowstorm blanketed the area. By the time he was reached, three days later, he was dead. As the rescue party was cutting the slings that had kept him secured to the mountain, his body slipped away over the side before anyone could do anything about it.[10]

Such are the tragedies that can, but fortunately seldom, overtake climbers in a high alpine environment such as the Bugaboos.

Crescent Towers at dusk - J.F. Garden

Bugaboo Spire and the Vowell Group - Roger W. Laurilla

The Howser Towers in evening light. From left to right they are the South Tower, Central Tower and North Tower - J.F. Garden

CHAPTER SEVEN:
High Angle Climbing

As the years advanced into the decade of the 1950's the sport of climbing continued to evolve. Technical climbing had come of age with the new innovations in aid climbing spreading worldwide.

Europeans were doing many fantastic things on the big walls of the Alps. However Americans would dominate the climbing scene in the Bugaboos for many years to come, well into the late 1960's.

Climbing, a sport pitting man against nature, also involves considerable competition within the climbing community. There is often rivalry between the best of climbers to be first to do a route or to push a route in greater style. Today the greatest challenges of mountaineering are to complete old aid routes in better style (without using aid) pushing the boundaries of what man is traditionally capable of climbing, or to conquer unclimbed walls, extending the limits beyond the vertical.

The development of technical aid climbing and the development of better protection had led to greater and greater feats. Many have claimed that technical aid climbing has been unnecessarily used to achieve first ascents and is, in essence, cheating! Others feel that the over-use of aid has led to tremendous advancements in rock-climbing technique, mainly due to that competitive spirit of doing something just a little better, a little faster or in more elegant style than the last climber. The basic grading of climbing difficulties has advanced as have the limits to which people are now climbing.

Aid climbing in the 50's was known as sixth class[1] in a grading scale of difficulty of one through five, six being impossible without aid. The advances in climbing, however, began to stretch the fifth grade considerably. What had previously been sixth grade was suddenly being climbed without aid! It is interesting in the modern day to see how far climbing has advanced. Many sixth grade climbs of the past are now considered no more than fifth grade – therein lies the challenge.

In the Bugaboos, the grading of climbs was initially established by those doing the climbing – the Americans. In California, Sierra climbers used a one to six grade scale to rate their climbing as well,

five being reserved for piton climbing, six for tension climbing. It was soon discovered that new climbing achievements were making a mockery of the established grading system, so a new open rating was established. Well known routes were selected and graded by the experts into an open-ended decimal system which could be better used to indicate specific difficulties on a climb. Initially scaled from 5.0 to 5.9, the fifth grade became, in this manner further defined to indicate the degree of free climbing to be encountered on a route. As an aid route was "pushed," and eventually climbed free, the fifth grade limits were extended out beyond 5.10 to, in modern day, perhaps 5.13.

Also added into the new grading system was a rating which determined the severity of the aid work required based on the European grading sytem of "A"1 and upwards. Rather than replacing the traditional grading sytem, the one to six scale is used to rate the overall difficulties of a climb in conjunction with a decimal system indicating severity of free climbing, and as well the amount of aid required on any particular climb. (See Appendix A). The decimal system became a uniform determination of difficulty. Theoretically, a 5.8 standard in the Bugaboos was the same as a 5.8 standard in Yosemite, all different factors taken into consideration. The important aspect of the decimal system was that it was an open-ended scale and could be extended as the limits of free climbing were pushed far beyond the expected.

In the 50's the Bugaboos were just beginning to see this extension of man's limits on the vertical granite walls. The big name hard men were just now discovering the potential of the Bugaboos as a rival to Yosemite or Colorado. Here were big walls in an alpine environment with all the added difficulties which only nature knew how to throw in.

On the Howser Spires there remained a peak unclimbed in 1955. In August of that year, a party of mountaineers consisting of George Austin, Jim McCarthy, John Rupley and David Bernays set their sights on that unclimbed summit – the Central Howser Tower.

On August 8, at the first light of dawn, they made

their approach to the mountain and the bergschrund guarding it. Purely by luck, they found a large block of snow bridging the gap, leaning against the upper lip of the 'schrund. Ice axes easily eradicated the roof, then came pitch after pitch of steep fluted ice and snow leading up towards the col between the Central and North Towers.

"The feeling of height was terrific," wrote David Bernays, "for we had underestimated the length and angle of the slope. The neighbouring peaks were already far below us and camp was just a collection of coloured dots amongst the rocks. We felt like tiny animals on a large and steep, white corrugated roof."[2]

After reaching the col, several pitches of rock led up to a sheer step and after searching desperately, a questionable chimney on the east side was given a go.

"It was more a vertical gulch than chimney, rotten, rickety, and very, very moist," Bernays described.[3]

After much difficulty and trepidation, the step was finally overcome and from that point it was an easy scramble to the summit. Amid threatening weather a descent was made, one long rappel being used to reach the 'schrund. Then, the heavens let loose with a celebration of thunderstorms.

In 1954 Jim McCarthy and John Rupley were in the Bugaboos and completed the first ascent of Pigeon Toe on July 29. From the Toe, they had taken a good hard look at route possibilities on the west face of Snowpatch, of which the only previous try was made by Gary Duggs back in 1953. Perseverence finally paid off in 1956 when McCarthy and Rupley again returned teaming up with Hans Kraus, an Austrian-American doctor whose credits included some very difficult climbing in the Alps and many new routes with Wiessner in the Shawangunks of New York State.

They were a strong climbing party, moving quickly up past McCarthy and Rupley's 1955 high point, alternating leads as they went. The route progressed very smoothly, the initial aid pitches going quite well up a long crack to a good belay point. Then the face eased off to a lesser angle, but

the choice of routes became difficult. There appeared to be two or three possibilities.

The decision was made to proceed left up a promising rib. Traversing that, another rib had to be negotiated, ascending to a belay point which required an extremely delicate step to reach. Kraus then led what was the key pitch. Climbing carefully over two ribs to an inside corner, the mountain became steeper, making friction work rather touchy.

"Hans was faced with the problem of doing a stirrup traverse under a ledge and then climbing over a bulging overhang," wrote McCarthy. "Carefully manipulating his stirrup and ropes to provide maximum protection and minimum drag, he started across. Working deftly and seemingly unaware of the steepness of the rock, he moved across the traverse and over the bulge in a triumph of sixth-class technique."[4]

Climbing upwards on a vertical crack, a layback and a traverse, the summit neared. A wide, insecure crack followed and ahead lay a narrow, slightly overhanging chimney which hindered manoeuvrability. Then some easy pitches led up on ledges to the summit itself, all attained in just eight and one half hours.

"The comparatively easy climb was the result of teamwork reached through long, continued practice," McCarthy reported.[5]

The face, though it appeared to be a rather difficult climb, succumbed much easier than anyone had thought possible. Perhaps the skill of the climbers made the ascent straight-forward, perhaps it was good teamwork. It was now obvious that the Bugaboo walls weren't as impossible as earlier consensus had it.

Bugaboo rock was excellent for hard climbing, solid and cohesive with tremendous friction on roughened granite. Climbers were becoming very adept with the techniques of aid climbing and hardened to the steepness and exposure which accompanied their exploits.

*Pigeon Spire, north face, with the Pigeon Toe on the left -
J.F. Garden*

Snowpatch Spire, west face. The Kraus-McCarthy route follows directly up the couloir just to the right of the south summit block - J.F. Garden

It was all coming together. Sooner or later the Bugaboo walls would succumb to the talents of the new rock climbers and here were some of the most challenging walls in North America.

In August of 1958, the first new route was placed on the Bugaboo Spire since Kain had first climbed it in 1916. This was to become a classic climb – the northeast ridge with a grading of III 5.7. John Rupley and Jim McCarthy had been on the northeast ridge (1956?) but were caught by a lightning storm, and were nearly pulled off a belay by a fall, so they retreated.

After a summer of challenging North American climbs including Ship Rock, Halett Peak, Grand Teton and Devil's Tower, climbers David Isles and Dick Sykes arrived in Boulder Camp where they teamed up with John Turner. Turner was an Englishman from Montreal who had completed many new climbs in the Adirondacks and Shawangunks. Another young American, Dave Craft joined the crew. They set out examining possibilities for new routes on the Bugaboo Spire and chose the northeast ridge as the likeliest.

During a reconnaissance, Turner and Isles explored between Bugaboo and Crescent Spires, examined the potential of the northeast ridge and proceeded to test a few pitches in the late afternoon. What they found was pleasing, good rock, straight forward climbing and an obvious line. But the day was late, so they returned to camp and enthusiastically convinced Sykes and Craft to join in the climb on the morrow.

August 8 dawned a perfect day. The climb progressed smoothly, most enjoyable for the climbers. Clean hard granite with excellent holds and cracks was all there was – it proved a winner![6] The 1,500 foot climb had taken only five hours on the ridge. It was an entirely free climb, requiring just a dozen pitons for protection.

Exploring a new route on the east face of Bugaboo Spire -
Rob Rohn

Towards the end of the 50's North America's best climbers were being attracted to the unscaled Bugaboo walls that presented some of the last great climbing problems on the continent outside of Alaska and the Yukon. During the next few years many interesting new routes and impressive face ascents would be recorded in the Bugaboos. The opportunities for such ascents were endless as the relief of the Bugaboo Spires provided possibilities of new routes from any and all angles.

Walls thought to be beyond climbing were ascended. Many attempts ended in frustration. Some climbs required more than a season before they finally succumbed. Perseverence became a virtue when for days or weeks the weather would close down. Climbers like Fred Beckey and Ed Cooper, who had the time and patience to accomplish what had never before been done, were the ones who enjoyed the satisfaction of defeating the Bugaboo challenge. The effort and determination of human beings pitted against nature led to the fame of the Bugaboo walls.

Alpine flowers along the trail - James B. Maitre

Above - East face of Bugaboo Spire - Glen Boles

Left - Northeast ridge and east face of Bugaboo Spire - Glen Boles

The northeast ridge of Bugaboo Spire with two teams of climbers ascending (circled) - J.F. Garden

Bugaboo Glacier and Snowpatch Spire - Roger W. Laurilla

Perched on an outcrop of rock directly above Boulder Camp and horizontally opposite the impressive east wall of Snowpatch Spire, two determined characters attired in knickers and wool shirts sat in the early morning light discussing the possibilities of climbing that east face. For Hank Mather and Fred Beckey the wall held great fascination and they were bound and determined to conquer it.

For many days in fine mid-July weather, they studied the sheer 2,050 foot face. The route they decided, would be a direct attack near the center of the face. The wall appeared slabby and crackless in the lower sections, but the top third, though still almost vertical, seemed to ease off somewhat with tilted slabs. The lower 800 feet, up to the elevation of the snowpatch, would be a massive and vertical undertaking with at least two major and some minor overhangs which would require aid. Above that the wall eases into a depression between the two summits. Belay points were examined through binoculars. Potential bivouac spots were picked out, and every crack on the proposed route studied. Pitching a tent on a moraine pile (surrounded by snow) not far from the face, equipment was sorted and selected, the plan being to force the route, day by day, returning to their tent until committed to the face. Once the climbers were too high to return to the comforts of their camp, a final push would be made with bivouacs on the face. Then would come the added risk of snowstorms, rain and lightning.

With the sun already behind the mountain on July 26, Beckey and Mather began the adventure. From the bergschrund at the base of the mountain a series of cracks began up the wall about five feet away, horizontally across the gap. Hank Mather, chortling at Beckey twirling on the end of the rope suspended in the 'schrund, belayed as Beckey tried to push himself off the névé wall reaching for the cracks in the granite of the east face. With much perseverance, a piton was attached and the assault began in earnest. Driving more angle pitons, Beckey navigated an overhang below Mather's belay position on the névé, using a new technique of self-tension. They worked for an hour establishing the start of the climb, then returned to their tent on the moraine for the night.

Dawn on July 27. Beckey tensioned back up the previous day's high position above the 'schrund and started working. After six hours of vertical efforts, he nearly fell in an exhausting attempt to push loose from a stirrup and mantle onto a thin two foot ledge intended for the first belay station. In a vertical distance of 160 feet, 40 pitons had been used. Some were homemade angles up to two or three inches. No such equipment as aluminum bongs or today's "Friends" yet existed. Next came the moss overhang which required complete defoliation in order to make the ascent.

Falling clear of the mountain straight down to the glacier, the moss littered the ice slope on the other side of the bergschrund. Once over the overhang, food, equipment and water were hauled up. Mather ascended, removing all the pitons save the ones below the overhang. Reaching the belay he did a layback up an inside right corner, a fifth class move for approximately 50 feet. Then more aid. After two hours Mather reached a platform large enough for one cheek. There he anchored himself well, fixed two ropes and rappelled down off the wall.

The next day was declared a rest day, so they returned to the valley for more pitons and extra gear. During the next two days they were on the wall again securing and reinforcing the route, moving their equipment upward. The third lead by Beckey, from the platform using double rope, was up some vertical cracks in an otherwise clean wall. Moss greatly delayed progress.

A series of problems confronted Beckey when faced with a difficult overhang where effective cracks were lacking. Exposure was fantastic. Moss clods whirred as they fell to the glacier. A rock buzzed by like a missile, far out from the face. Hank Mather led the fourth lead, a most difficult and awkward one. Cracks were often insufficient, rotten and full of moss. This section, known as the White overhang, was vertical and uncompromising and had to be left unfinished as darkness prevailed.

After hauling equipment and working the east face on the morning of July 29, Beckey and Mather decided to give it up for the time being. They wandered around Snowpatch to the west face where their planned descent would take place should they succeed on the east face. There they were able to climb all but the last 300 feet of the mountain that afternoon.

On July 30, they again returned up the east face of Snowpatch, but nothing seemed to go according to form. Disillusioned with the slowness of their third and fourth leads they agreed to retreat. Back on the glacier Beckey and Mather resolved to do the west face again, this time to the top. They both needed a rest from the stress associated with working a wall such as the east face. Continuous exposure and difficulty were beginning to tell.

Mountain fireweed and Broad-leafed Arnica - J.F. Garden

Snowpatch Spire at sunrise. The route Beckey and Mather climbed begant just right of the snow fan and angled almost directly to the south summit - J.F. Garden

Bugaboo Spire at sunrise. The route up this east face, climbed by Cooper and Gran, goes up to the large ledge conspicuous near the bottom, then straight up direct to the north summit - J.F. Garden

Snowpatch from Bugaboo Spire - James B. Maitre

Fred Beckey and Hank Mather's perception of rest was somewhat different from the norm. Rest to them was nothing other than tackling another route, one that was preferably unclimbed! With two friends they again went after the west face of Snowpatch. This would be only the third ascent of the face (although a new route). Accompanying Mather and Beckey were Brian Greenwood, a young English-born climber from Calgary, and Elfrida Pigou who became the first woman to climb Snowpatch Spire.

The four set off early on the morning of July 31 and followed up a trough system on the great slabs of the west face of Snowpatch to the central notch between the north and south summit. Fresh snow had fallen overnight hampering progress beyond Beckey and Mather's previous high point.

Using several bolts, Fred Beckey awkwardly committed himself on moist granite, finally forcing a passage up the route. A nice pendulum lead by Mather to the summit ridge notch resulted in success just as the sun descended. Making good time to the north summit a quick rappel was completed down the shadowy slabs to the base of the mountain. The party arrived back in camp not long after dark.

On August 5, after a week of bad weather, parties of climbers set off from Boulder Camp as the sky dawned clear and bright. Beckey and Mather longed to go at the east face route on Snowpatch again. Ed Cooper, who was also in camp, teamed up with Elfrida Pigou for an attempt that day on the west face of Bugaboo Spire. Cooper had been working with Art Gran on the spectacular east face of Bugaboo Spire for three days. That attempt took them within 500 feet of the summit before a bivouac in a snowstorm forced them off the mountain. Cooper had been in the Bugaboos during 1958 and at that time laid plans to return again in 1959 with his sights set on one of the big walls. Beckey and Mather were already on the east face of Snowpatch, so Cooper and Gran planned to attempt Bugaboo Spire's east wall.

Prior to attempting Bugaboo's east face, Cooper,

Gran and Roman Sadowy conquered the north face of Anniversary Peak for the first time. The 2,000 foot crescent-shaped ice slope referred to as a sickle snowslope, rose from the Bugaboo Glacier tongue and ended 300 feet east of the summit. It was an easy climb, the upper slopes steepening to 45 degrees with hard ice under the snow cover. Traversing over to Howser Peak, Kain's first ascent signature was brought down with them. Now with Pigou, Cooper set his sights on another first ascent – the west face of Bugaboo Spire.

On a reconnaissance of the west face days earlier Cooper discovered some grisly remains. At the base of the west face on a large talus fan were ". . .an old pair of rotted climbing boots together with a few bones. This was perhaps the remains of the unfortunate lightning accident just below the summit of Bugaboo Spire in 1948. The body, which fell down the 2500 foot face was never found at that time."[1]

Not realizing what he had discovered on the talus slope, Ed Cooper had no qualms about pursuing the first ascent of Bugaboo Spire's west face. Initially, Cooper and Pigou followed a large diagonal ledge for some 600 feet, fresh snow and verglas made everything tricky. From the long ledge, a traverse up to the left was made to a large prominent shelf which can be easily seen on the west face. Straight up from the shelf the climb led to a 120 degree overhang inside a chimney, the only pitch requiring direct aid on the entire climb. Above that, another diagonal ledge was reached leading up to the base of the Great White Wall, 1500 feet of 90 degree smooth, white, rotten granite.

"The ledge led on to a ridge," Cooper wrote. "We dropped slightly down on the other side of the ridge into a wide, shallow gully. The west face of Bugaboo is quite complex with many minor ridges and gullies. At this point we climbed upward many hundreds of feet and slightly to the right to what we thought was a subsidiary ridge of the west face, but was the south ridge itself, just below the gendarme and some 250 feet from the summit. In less than half an hour we were at the south summit watching the setting sun. Return to camp was long after dark."[2]

August snowstorm - Rob Rohn

The climb itself had been grade III to IV with one section requiring aid below the Great White Wall. One week later, Beckey with Pete Geiser and Roman Sadowy climbed the same face, only this time straight up to the summit rather than to the south ridge. Since this route was held to be more direct than Cooper's, Beckey was credited with the first ascent of the west face."[3]

Meanwhile on the morning of August 5, while Cooper and Pigou were on the Bugaboo west face, Mather and Beckey began their final ascent bid on the east face of Snowpatch. Easily reaching their previous high point by climbing fixed ropes they had left in place, Mather was able to complete the problematic fourth pitch, ending it in a stirrup belay in the confines of a smooth-walled chimney.

Beckey followed and led pitch five with some free climbing to a ledge and an inside aid corner above, ending in a hanging belay. Mather again took over, working until dark on the most difficult problem of the climb, ominously dubbed the Black overhang. He prepared the overhang for the next morning's assault, placed several 3/16 inch bolts on the overhang and retreated to a previously-passed ledge where a sleepless but relaxing night was spent.

The temperature dipped below freezing as dawn broke on August 6th. Running water had frozen the fixed ropes which Mather had left in place. Prusiking back up was difficult. Hands were cold, the pain excruciating!

Mather tensioned up the Black overhang, led up a solitary crack above, then bolted into the wall to pull up the loads. With great difficulty and delay, everything was finally over the Black overhang by 4 p.m. After this pitch, the wall changed drastically with occasional free-climbing.

The worst was over and the climbing became less desperate, though still difficult fifth class on the wall. With some strenuous moments, five and a half vigorous leads were made before darkness. The weather now threatened, but it was too late to retreat. The summit was now within reach.

A cold bivouac was made on a tiny snowpatch and granite sandpile on a 30 degree slab. Next morning, August 7, a final push to the summit was completed. It was largely free climbing, good cracks allowing fast progress. Shortly past noon Beckey and Mather reached the summit, after five days of effort, some 160 pitons, eight bolts, and a few wooden wedges.[4]

Descent was via their new west face route. They retrieved fixed ropes on the lower east face before leaving the wall for the last time.

"It had been one of the greatest adventures of our lives..." concluded Fred Beckey.[5]

Climbers on the east face of Snowpatch Spire - J.F. Garden

Northeast ridge of Snowpatch Spire - Glen Boles

Anniversary Peak and Hound's Tooth - James B. Maitre

Bugaboo Spire showing the west ridge route and to the right, the east face - J.F. Garden

CHAPTER NINE:
Cooper's East Faces

During the summer of 1959, while Fred Beckey was struggling with the east face of Snowpatch Spire, an equally dramatic and difficult struggle took place on the east face of the Bugaboo Spire. Its chief actor was Ed Cooper, friend and climbing companion of Beckey. Cooper might have been on Snowpatch with Beckey and Mather had he not been engaged in his own epic adventure.

Cooper's companion on the east face expedition was Art Gran, an easterner of considerable repute as a hard man in the Shawangunks of New York State. Cooper and Gran had known each other in their home state of New York, but neither had known of the other's Bugaboo plans until they met at Boulder Camp.

They began a long and arduous challenge which, it turned out, would require two seasons to accomplish. For two days in 1959, Cooper and Gran worked to pioneer a route on the east face of Bugaboo Spire from directly below the north summit. On the third day they were forced off the mountain by the same storm which halted Beckey and Mather on the east face of Snowpatch.

Frustrated by the weather, they left fixed ropes and turned to other plans. (Cooper's Bugaboo west face ascent with Elfrida Pigou and a solo climb of Snowpatch via Bedayn's route.) On August 6 they were able to return to the face. On that very cold morning, the ropes were coated in ice and nothing went right.

Cooper and Gran reascended to their previous high point and began working through a chimney to a large ledge which they traversed up to an inside corner. Rocks were continually plummeting down, unnerving both climbers. At this point they were confronted with three possible routes of ascent. They took the right hand lead of the three possible lines, but it ended abruptly. They therefore tried the middle line utilizing a 100 foot pendulum into the center of the face. Then the bolt kit broke. By 10 p.m. they aborted the climb. On their descent, after reaching the bergschrund at 4 a.m., Gran was struck by falling rock and knocked down the snow slope leading out from the base of the mountain. So ended the first attempt!

In July 1960, Ed Cooper returned, determined to stay as long as necessary to finish the climb he and Art Gran had started on Bugaboo Spire's east face. He drove from Seattle in a disreputable 1952 power-glide Chevy, his pocket light with five dollars. In the back of the Chevy was a load of scrounged surplus provisions.

On his own, he packed his meagre supplies and equipment into Boulder Camp, loads which included 800 feet of rope for fixed lines, and a 70 foot aid sling for solo climbing. Up he went to the Balcony, a ledge 250 feet up a vertical grade V chimney on the face. Then a week of bad weather set in and down he came. When good days finally appeared, Cooper again returned to the east face.

From the Balcony, 200 feet of easy climbing on a left traverse led him to the real problems.

"The first lead of V plus went easily enough," Cooper wrote, "although it offered one short artificial section, where I fixed a rope. I now studied the next lead, the 'Black Stain' pitch, as this was the lead I feared the most. I climbed an overhung chimney until I had to swing out onto the narrow, overhanging right edge. My stirrups kept slipping off and I swung under to the right or to the left. I was quite ready to call it a day after this long, exhausting artificial pitch."[1]

Ropes were fixed and a descent made to the Balcony.

The next day Cooper progressed to a point some 1000 feet higher over leads that, though requiring some aid, were certainly less demanding than the first day's efforts. After descending once again to the Balcony, this time for equipment, Cooper reascended to his highest point where there was a ledge-of-sorts. There he bivouaced for the night.

"From this point there are three possible lines," wrote Cooper, "all along dihedrals leading to easier ground higher up. The left one reaches easy ground the soonest, but like the middle one is difficult of access. It is for this reason that we had selected the one to the right on our attempt of the previous summer, but we found to our dismay that it led into a 'cul-de-sac' of overhangs."[2]

As morning light flooded the face "...I started placing bolts immediately above the bivouac in an attempt to reach the middle dihedral. Twelve bolts later, in the late afternoon of the third full day on the face, I reached a chimney that led to it."[3]

The drill he was using became useless as it stuck in the holder. The twelfth hole was the last possible. The drill had to be broken three times in order to sharpen it, a method which worked surprisingly well.

With his piton hammer disintegrating and food in short supply, Cooper descended the face over his fixed lines to the glacier in one hour. Then he made for Boulder camp where again, as in 1959, he met up with Art Gran.

Gran relates... "In 1960 Ed and I met again in the Bugaboos 'called by this lovely mountain.' He had arrived first and had put in fixed ropes to a point 350 feet below our 1959 high point...a brilliant job of solo climbing."[4]

After a week of bad weather Gran and Cooper were able to ascend the fixed ropes to Cooper's high point. Starting a new lead at 9 a.m., they worked up a long narrow and difficult chimney which took until 2 p.m. to negotiate. The top of the middle dihedral was gained from that chimney, then three long leads of artificial climbing up a corner brought them within striking distance of the summit and much easier climbing.

Thinking the worst was over... "In gathering darkness and deteriorating weather, we hurried to a large ramp leading to the east ridge, 100 feet below the summit. We were momentarily stunned to find a 40 foot vertical wall at the end of the ramp. Art did a beautiful job leading this aid pitch in the inky blackness of the night," wrote Cooper, "feeling the size of the crack with his fingers and then choosing the piton accordingly. In the end we had to bivouac on a small ledge right on the ridge, miserably cold and watching lightning on distant peaks."[5]

Gran meanwhile describes the final near-summit bivouac... "A bolt of lightning struck a peak to the west and we got jumpy. It reminded us that a whole party had been killed by lightning on this

same mountain only a few years before. We decided to climb on if another bolt struck, but there was no more lightning so we remained in bivouac."[6]

Cooper described the victory. "At 6:30 a.m. we stood on the summit feeling numb rather than elated."[7]

So ended one of the most determined efforts to defeat an impossible wall. Cooper's solo effort of 1960 would have been an incredible achievement had he completed it alone, but as most of the work of route finding had been done with Gran in 1959, he did not hesitate to enlist Gran's help for the final bid. The east face is a quite barren wall, leaning at an approximate angle of 85 degrees for 1800 vertical feet. The new route, which is now normally a two-day climb, required 2010 feet of roped climbing, of which 280 feet was direct aid with some 100 pitons used. Descent was made by the Kain route. At the col it started snowing again and didn't let up for five days. On the third day, in the snow, Cooper and Gran recovered most of the ropes off the face though two were stuck. Cooper was later able to remove them.

Today, the great challenge of the east face is to climb Cooper's route, the only route, using no aid whatsoever. His climb requires moves on the order of 5.10!

That same summer of 1960 saw a number of interesting climbs accomplished by many noteworthy climbers, all this despite rather poor weather conditions. Besides Ed Cooper and Art Gran, others made their presence felt in the Bugaboos: Yvon Chouinard, Ken Weeks, Claude Suhl, George Bloom, Bill Sanders and Layton Kor.

"Almost everyone did Snowpatch and most of the other standard routes," wrote Art Gran. "Kor and Suhl did the east ridge of Bugaboo Spire in four hours. Sanders and I, Suhl and Bloom did Snowpatch in five hours from the meadows."[8]

East face of Bugaboo Spire - Ed Cooper

Colorado stone mason Layton Kor, was an up-and-coming figure in the world of rock climbing. During 1959, he succeeded in putting the first route on the famous east wall of Longs Peak, the Diagonal, with Ray Northcutt. In the summer of 1960 in the Bugaboos, he showed a strong, ambitious climbing style by mastering a number of new routes there. With Bill Sanders he completed a route on Eastpost Spire's south face and after a treacherous crossing of the Bugaboo Glacier icefall an ascent of Marmolata Hound's Tooth by the northeast face. Most impressive of all was his and partner Claude Suhl's ascent of Bugaboo Spire's north face, a 2000 foot series of long granite slabs. The first 600 feet of the climb was an obvious route leading over fourth class ledges and cracks to a more difficult wall which surges up at an angle of 75 degrees. At the base of the steep wall, a long traverse was made into the center of the face. Working their way upwards they found themselves in a difficult and questionable position.

To overcome the clean face confronting them, expansion bolts were placed, and though Kor experienced a 15 foot fall while leading, they were able to traverse right into a more feasible series of cracks. Working up those cracks for three rope lengths, then up a right diagonal line, they emerged on the east ridge route half a rope-length below the north summit.

"The climb took nine hours and about 45 pitons were required," wrote Kor, "including 18 for belay points. Three pitons, and two bolts were used for aid."[9] This was a very fast climb over an extremely exposed face, the sort of climbing Layton Kor was soon to become renowned for.

Kor was not about to quit with that success and on August 16 he teamed up with Ed Cooper and they established the classic east face route on Pigeon Spire.

Bugaboo Spire as viewed from the Vowell Glacier. The north face that Kor and Suhl ascended is on the right side of the mountain - Roger W. Laurilla

Pigeon is a beautiful peak especially when viewed from eastward exposures. Its most obvious feature are the massive series of slabs which angle steeply upward from the Warren icefall. Above the slabs the mountain pitches straight up with a clean vertical wall before somewhat higher and easier slopes lead to the pointed summit.

Rapidly climbing to the lower left corner of the east face, Kor and Cooper began their climb up the spire. The first 1000 feet progressed over fantastically smooth 60 degree slabs. Following cracks and ledges over the slabs they climbed 300 feet on a right diagonal line to a large ledge which crossed the face. Following that to its extreme end, another 400 feet were ascended on a left diagonal line until it was possible to traverse back right to the base of a left diagonal roof. The roof was climbed in two direct aid leads using a stirrup belay. After two more pitches of free climbing they found themselves on top of a giant slab, a pedestal from which Cooper managed a pendulum traverse to a crack on the right of the wall.

After a very difficult and delicate lead, Cooper climbed up to a belay spot and assisted Kor.[10] Next was an inside right corner of strenuous difficulty, then easier climbing which led over a short face to the right hand ridge. Reaching the summit some 300 feet higher, they were greeted by snowflakes. Eight and one half hours and 55 pitons were needed to reach the top – an excellent climb on beautiful rock, in keeping with the Bugaboo tradition.[11]

Pigeon Spire, east face - J.F. Garden

Facing page - East face of Pigeon Spire - Glen Boles

Facing page, left -Layton Kor on the east face of Pigeon Spire - Ed Cooper

The rounded grooves on Pigeon Spire, east face - Roger W. Laurilla

Glen Boles
85'

CHAPTER TEN:
Patagonia

The summer of 1961 was a busy and satisfying period in Fred Beckey's climbing life. During this summer he completed 34 ascents and 26 new routes, mostly in the Pacific Northwest. Travelling to Canada, Beckey attempted Mt. Robson's north face with Ed Cooper – a 2000 foot snow and ice face. The day after their attempt, the face was wiped clean by an avalanche, proving the very delicate balance of timing in climbing achievements. Teaming up with Yvon Chouinard and Dan Doody, Beckey successfully climbed the dangerous north face of Mt. Edith Cavell near Jasper. Then Chouinard and Beckey alone went on to climb the north face of Mt. Sir Donald in the Selkirks.

In the Bugaboos, Beckey's attention turned to the unexplored walls of the Howser Spires and with Chouinard, he began scouting the possibilities. The Bugaboos were, by 1961, becoming a rock climber's mecca, yet there were many unclimbed walls and route possibilities. Siege tactics of years gone by were now outdated. Accomplishments by Beckey and Cooper were overshadowed by the newer Yosemite methods and the technique of pushing routes up in one grand effort.

Fixed ropes became a thing of the past. Fast, free climbing, avoiding aid where possible was the modern method. Yvon Chouinard experimented with and developed new equipment which altered climbing styles considerably.

Summer 1961 saw many climbers and much activity in the Bugaboos. Art Gran was back. With John Hudson, he completed a new and difficult 5.7 route on the west face of Snowpatch. But it was Fred Beckey and Yvon Chouinard who made the greatest contributions in the continuing exploration of the vertical world of the Bugaboos.

On the morning of August 5, Beckey and Chouinard were camped at Pigeon col, and though their minds were set on the big walls of the South Howser Tower, they couldn't resist trying a new route on the north face of Pigeon spire. Across the 'schrund and up an 80 foot direct aid crack they went. Ascending slabs to a wide singular crack

Howsers in storm - U. Veideman

which was the only feasible route, they reached a trying overhang and halted. Threatening weather suspended their attempt and they rappelled off, returning the next day.

Prusiking up ropes they had left during that retreat proved difficult as everything was coated in ice. Chouinard led up the long aid pitch over the difficult overhang, reaching an enjoyable layback which led to a good belay point. Next came a vertical inside corner with jutting holds that appeared loose but were in fact solid. Two more easy leads followed and they were on the prominent summit ice patch in early afternoon. Beckey relates, "the most interesting recollection of this climb was that some character (a friend of mine whose name is Miller) shouted up to us from the glacier in pseudo-French and carried on a conversation with us. He told us he was Rebuffat. We believed this bluff and did more shouting. Later we learned who he was and were pretty amused by the whole episode."

Their thoughts now focused on the challenge of South Howser Tower. "The conquest of the great western buttress of the Howser Spires remains the greatest alpine challenge in the Bugaboos," wrote Fred Beckey. "Perhaps the most classically beautiful route lies up the west buttress of the South Tower."[1] The Howser Spires had seen little activity since 1941 even though the Howsers are the highest of the Bugaboos. The visible eastern side was seldom climbed and the western side, hidden to all, was almost totally unknown.

In 1959 Beckey and friends did visit the western side and they explored the faces for possible routes. The spectacular granite walls they found reminded them of Patagonia: giant columns of rock soaring 2000 feet or more resembling a North American version of Fitzroy or Cerro Torre.[2] They explored the first 300 feet of the most prominent west buttress of South Howser Tower with its clean lines and vertical grace.

Examining a possible route, the initial third of the line appeared conventional enough with several crack systems leading upward on clean sloping slabs, then a section of broken rock led directly to a steep lichen free wall of white granite; split by a single crack: the Great White Headwall.

The final section then looked rather easy above that, but inclement weather prevented any serious attempts in 1959. Beckey considered this a climb of the highest Yosemite standards.

Returning in August of 1961, Fred Beckey was again staring at the west face of the South Howser Tower, set upon completing the first ascent of this immense pillar of granite. With him was the now famous climbing technologist, Yvon Chouinard. Three weeks earlier they had completed the first ascent of the north face of Mt. Edith Cavell. Then they had set out to prepare for the climb on South Howser carrying ropes, food and other equipment to the base of the pillar on August 7.

"Chouinard was very optimistic that we could force the climb in two days; we took along enough food and water for two and one half days as well as our bivouac gear and a carefully selected stock of Chouinard pitons and carabiners, bolt kit and stirrups," wrote Beckey in the American Alpine Journal.[3]

Exploring two pitches, they returned to camp leaving fixed ropes in place for the next day's serious start of the climb.

As the morning light began to touch on the upper ramparts of South Howser Tower, Beckey and Chouinard ascended the two pitches they had explored the previous day. To Chouinard's horror, as he arrived at the upper ledge where the ropes were tied off, he noticed the nylon lines were almost completely frayed or chewed through. Stepping out of his prusik slings, the realization of near disaster struck him. He had entrusted his life to a rope which had been attacked by the ever voracious mountain rodents – packrats, sometimes more commonly called snafflehounds. The loss of the rope failed to thwart their ambitions though, and climbing proceeded in earnest to the base of the Great White Headwall. Initially, climbing was difficult though not artificial, but on the second step of the buttress some aid climbing became necessary. Then on to the third step where there were two more difficult leads on laybacks on a dihedral, then three more leads over a series of blocks to the base of the Great White Headwall.

Jam cracks and laybacks on perfect granite, excellent belay positions; a most enjoyable climb. The use of Chouinard's newly developed bong-bongs and Bugaboo pitons proved ideal on this very esthetic wall. That day they accomplished 13 pitches of climbing, eight of which were free 5.4 or 5.5 climbing. For the night they rappelled back down to a . . . "small sandy spot incredibly perfect for a bivouac."[4]

Morning broke with ominous skies overhead. Working their way back to the exposed headwall, Beckey noted "the exposure and the starkness of the route at this point becomes unique, as one is climbing on the narrow headwall between the terrible drop to the north couloir and the sweep of the great south face."[5]

The headwall was climbed in two direct-aid pitches nailing 16 pitons up a single narrow crack with a true hanging belay in stirrups. Thirteen more pitons led into a chimney on the right which eventually opened up into free climbing.

On the twentieth pitch a difficult 40 feet were overcome in a chimney past a prominent block, then they nailed up the left wall of a dihedral chimney using knife blade pitons. Free climbing followed up delicate cracks and along a sharp arête. By mid-afternoon Beckey and Chouinard were on the summit, reached over easy fourth class climbing and scrambling.

"In addition to anchors," wrote Beckey, "the ascent had taken 135 pitons; no bolts were used and no pitons were left behind."[6]

The excellent rock, Chouinard's new devices and aids, and the skill and determination of the two climbers enabled the first ascent of this classic route to be completed without the use of bolts. Since then, the route has been climbed entirely free with 5.8 and 5.9 leads and has become a classic rock route, perhaps the finest free route in Canada.

South Tower of the Howsers from the west - Roger W. Laurilla

For Fred Beckey and Yvon Chouinard, once the tricky descent was made to Pigeon Col and Boulder Camp reached, it was a pleasure to relax and celebrate with friends. Their accomplishments, though since surpassed, are by no means any the less, for theirs was the pioneering ascent of a wall which no one else had been able to climb.

The next day they were off again, this time to look at the sheer rock and ice face of the east side of South Howser Tower. They scrambled fairly high up the face but were not prepared to commit themselves to a summit attempt.

Early on the morning of August 11 Beckey and Chouinard began a determined ascent of the east face of South Howser Tower. Across the 'schrund and up the ice slope they proceeded, then a long vertical crack was followed on the left side of a rock flake that divides the hanging ice slope above the 'schrund. That had been their high point on the previous day. From there Chouinard traversed across shattered rock. He resorted to rappelling into the steep hanging ice wall on the right. Retreat now seemed impossible.

The next leads continued up a 55 degree ice slope where an exit appeared. Rubble to begin with, it became beautiful granite then narrowed into a jam-crack.

"A pure vertical diedre needed two pitons for stirrups; otherwise the lower half of the face was extremely enjoyable though strenuous fifth class," Beckey wrote.[7] Up a cleft in the face to where it divided, direct-aid was required to surmount a short wall – either that or a treacherous ice patch where ice and rockfall were beginning to come down. Upward they climbed to a 125 foot wall that had good layback holds and piton cracks.

The Beckey-Chouinard route on South Howser Tower follows directly up the vertical ridge seen in profile, to the summit - J.F. Garden

Beckey and Chouinard climbed directly up the centre of the east face of South Howser Tower, almost directly above the righthand climber seen crossing below - J.F. Garden

Tufted Fleabane - J.F. Garden

Beckey reported in the Canadian Alpine Journal that... "the crux move was a severe arm workout on an overhanging flake that had skylight on its inside. We then climbed a slab wall right, a gully left, and on the last lead, a purely enjoyable slab-ramp took me to the summit blocks. The climb had taken about six hours from camp."[8]

The descent was made over the original, normal route. And so ended the accomplishments of the 1961 climbing season in the Bugaboos. "Of all the Bugaboo peaks, the fabulous South Tower has been woefully neglected by climbers, and only this year had seen the first climb in 20 years. It was the only Bugaboo peak with but one route," wrote Beckey.[9] The Howser Towers were coming into focus as the last of the great problems, the actual west wall of the highest North Howser Tower, was yet unclimbed.

Fred Beckey's climbing successes were becoming phenomenal. He was having a difficult time finding permanent climbing companions; his pace of achievement was unrelenting, his drive reflecting the nature of the man. The vertical granite ramparts of Howser's western wall beckoned him; Beckey was not yet through with his adventures in the Bugaboos.

CHAPTER ELEVEN:
Beckey Returns

In 1963 Fred Beckey made two visits to the Bugaboos. On his first stop in early July a tremendous amount of snow still filled the couloirs and adorned the ledges of the Bugaboo Spires. Despite the inclement conditions on the peaks, Beckey and Steve Marts were able to climb the southeast face of Pigeon Spire for the first time.

On July 2, climbing the glacier slopes to the left of the great eastern slabs on Pigeon, Beckey and Marts decided to attempt the buttress-like face between the eastern slabs and the south face. This face was as yet unclimbed. Thin cracks starting from the corner between the slanting ledge systems of the south face and slabs of the east face appeared to lead high on the spire, perhaps offering a new and classic Bugaboo route up Pigeon.

The climb began with a difficult overhang using aid up an open book-end, making a hanging belay necessary at the top of the pitch. Beckey proceeded over another overhang and up a flaky crack to the first ledge in 300 feet. Going to the right and up two more flakes, a two-foot ledge was found that would be the bivouac spot, though before dark a long solitary crack was ascended up a smooth wall leaving a fixed rope in place.

On July 3 Beckey and Marts left their bivouac and prusiked up their fixed ropes. The difficulties began immediately. Three pitches required either direct aid using giant bongs, or very hard free climbing. However, the summit was reached by mid-morning after three pitches of more reasonable climbing. The southeast face of Pigeon Spire now had a new route. This was the only climbing of note in the Bugaboos that July because of the excessive amount of snow on all the other spires.

At times, snow remains in the Bugaboos well into July. Located as they are directly in the westerly storm tracks of moisture laden Pacific air, the Spires receive a fair share of snow. This is compounded by the jutting vertical profile which exceeds that of all the nearby ranges.

Pigeon Spire from the north. Beckey and Marts climbed the north face directly below the prominent snowpatch seen under the summit - J.F. Garden

Two Austrian-Canadians, Hans Gmoser and Leo Grillmair, took note of this liberal snowfall and the obvious beauty of the area. During the winter of 1963-64 they set in motion their dream to make a livelihood in the Bugaboos, guiding people on ski tours of this vertical granite wilderness. The dream was to become a great success. The Bugaboo name was to become synonymous with powder skiing, as it had already been associated with rock climbing.

For some then, the Bugaboos have become a year-round playground with untapped recreational possibilities.

After the climb on Pigeon Spire, and because of the late snow conditions, Beckey did not linger in the Bugaboos. However he wrote of his continuing romance with the region, "...the one climb that haunted me was the great western wall of its highest summit, Howser Spire. Estimates of its height had run from 3000 to 5000 feet, but actually it is probably a bit under the former. Yet, it is the highest precipice in the range and until Brian Greenwood and I climbed it on August 5, perhaps its outstanding unclimbed challenge."[1]

And so Beckey found time to return again in 1963 to the Bugaboos where he teamed up with Canadian climber Brian Greenwood to begin the final great problem of the Howsers.

Rising out of the rubble deposited by two hanging glaciers, the west face of Howser Spire towers upward to a pair of great points or steps. On the left, waterfalls descend from one hanging glacier. On the right, great slabs of granite plate the face that connects the buttress with the hanging glacier between Howser and the South Tower. A narrow snow couloir provides a niche in the armour of the lower buttress. Greenwood and Beckey decided to pursue that avenue.

By noon August 4 they had ascended the couloir and rocks above, reaching the first step or break in the buttress. Direct aid on wet rock provided some difficulties, but surmounting that and a short rappel down a slanting snow and ice corner, the foot of the final wall was reached in late afternoon. They went up very exposed ice, on a crack system

on the northern corner of the buttress, then retreated to a tiny ledge where a bivouac spot was established before dark.

A clear morning found Beckey and Greenwood prusiking back up to their high point, then again working their way up the crack system they had been following. Direct aid was nearly continuous for some distance before reaching the first ledge in the system. Some tedious and very slow free climbing followed as a result of verglas and snow in the cracks, but most of the technical climbing was complete although the mountain yet had many obstacles en route to the summit.

Giant blocks of granite frozen together by ice required careful work. Within several hundred feet of the summit a long ice traverse, treacherously covered with loose snow had to be negotiated to bypass a badly pinnacled knife edge. This blocked the route to the top.

"Looking down, it seemed like a version of the Eigerwand," wrote Fred Beckey, "with all the ice and loose snow plastered on the route. We climbed to the summit in the moonlight, and then built a bivouac platform of loose rocks to spend a second night out. In the morning we happily descended the north ridge to the Vowell Glacier."[2]

New routes with a more direct line and up more difficult sections of the western wall of the Howsers were certainly to follow Beckey and Greenwood's achievement. Theirs was a first, however. Others would follow and outdo what they had done, but the greatest effort was the pioneering climb.

Once a route is established others invariably follow up the pioneering adventure by pushing themselves and their climbing abilities on the route. After the first ascent, the challenge becomes one of doing the route in better time and with less or no aid. Thus the limits of climbing are forever being extended, even though climbs may be repeated over and over again.

Fred Beckey knew the challenge, the pleasure of extending his skills on the mountain and the joy of attaining his goals. He was fortunate to be in the Bugaboos when there were yet many first ascents to be done. Without question he was a true pioneer of mountaineering. The 1966 edition of <u>Appalachia</u> reported that Fred Beckey's all-round mountaineering feats have never been exceeded by anyone in the history of North American mountaineering. He had, at that time, 500 new routes and first ascents to his credit. To this day Fred Beckey is still very active in his sport, often climbing with people half his age. His achievements in the Bugaboos of British Columbia have brought fame not only to his climbing skills and determination, but to the Spires themselves.

West face, Howser Towers - Glen Boles

The first climb of the North Howser Tower on the west face by Beckey and Greenwood followed the far left buttress starting in a narrow snow couloir - Scott Flavelle

CHAPTER TWELVE:
Traverse

August 1965. Huddled under boulders of granite, four climbers whiled away the hours playing cards or reading books. Rain and sleet obliterated the sky. For four days they waited, bored and despondent. Finally the weather broke, they gathered their gear, prepared their equipment, and began the climb.

Yvon Chouinard led, followed by Eric Rayson, Jock Lang and Doug Tompkins. Their intent was an epic traverse of the entire three peaks of the Howser Towers from north to south. If successful not only would they achieve the first traverse of the massif, but also the first ascent of the direct north face of South Howser Tower.

Yvon Chouinard, from southern California, a veteran of Yosemite and an extremely competent climbing technician, possessed all the merits and drive to lead this unheard of traverse attempt. With successes on the North American Wall and Muir Wall of El Capitan, the north face of Mount Edith Cavell; his fame as writer and critic of the mountaineering world; his inventiveness in the design and construction of climbing equipment, Chouinard has pursued his "search for the ultimate experience."[1] In the Bugaboos, he had previously climbed with Fred Becky ascending South Howser Tower by the east and west faces. Now he and his friends were determined to achieve the most ambitious project in the annals of the Bugaboos.

On day one, the quartet of climbers ascended the moderately steep icefield north of the North Tower, climbing separately in pairs, utilizing crampons and protecting with ice-axe belays. The rocks of the mountain were reached by mid-morning and the summit of the North Tower by late afternoon.

After a warm bivouac, day two began with the ascent of the Central Tower. Long rappels were required to reach the notch between the Central and South Tower, a cold and inhospitable place. Direct aid began immediately from the notch on their new ascent of the South Tower, nailing up five pitches of the northeast arête to what appeared might be easier ground.

Several difficult fifth class pitches were approached in steps and as night came on, the last difficulty encountered. "After placing a knife blade in total darkness," Doug Tompkins related, "he (Eric Rayson) stepped into a sling suspended from it (the piton) to reach a jam crack leading upwards. We were amazed to watch him use in the crack, like a pair of brass knuckles, a two-inch bong that had holes to lighten it. Eventually he stepped onto the bong to surmount the difficulty. Unfortunately the ledge he had reached was big enough for only one person and so we fixed ropes and descended to a larger ledge some hundred feet lower for a bivouac."[2]

After another pleasant night on the mountain the party began their third day. Optimistically expecting to spend a day and a half on the traverse, they had brought only enough food for that length of time. Now they were perilously short. A lack of food meant a shortage of energy and subsequently, weakness. Safety in a climb often requires individual strength and the weaker one gets, the more likely a stumble or slip might occur. They had to complete the traverse and be off the mountain that day!

The summit of the South Tower was reached by mid-morning and the descent begun.

"We spiraled off the tower in some six rappels, a routine but time-consuming process. The last one deposited us onto the glacier at about 3 o'clock," chronicled Tompkins.[3]

Though somewhat of an ordeal and certainly a climb that required more effort and time than they had calculated, Tompkins reported they had experienced "one of the finest alpine climbs in North America, for all aspects of mountaineering had been brought into play from third to sixth class, from rappels to traverses, from ice climbing to technical rock climbing. It tested all the skills. It was not hazardous, nor was it easy, but rather it was enjoyable in the difficulties it presented."[4]

This expedition ended the greatest era of pioneering climbs in the Bugaboos. In the 25 years from 1940 to 1965 the unclimbed peaks and walls of the Bugaboos have succumbed to the aspirations of relentless individuals, some of whom have returned again and again to meet the challenge that these extreme vertical walls have presented.

The Bugaboos, though awesomely beautiful in their vertical relief, are a mountain group undeniably bound to the personalities who have invaded the area since Conrad Kain's day. The Bugaboos may no longer be the prime wilderness and unspoiled landscape that Fred Beckey or Raffi Bedayn first enjoyed. Perhaps though, that continuing fame and world renown may help to preserve and protect the area, and others, from the ravages of civilization.

Howser Towers from Bugaboo Spire - J.F. Garden

Pigeon Spire in morning light - Ed Cooper

Mountain meadows in the Bugaboos - Ed Cooper

'Energy Crisis', Crescent Spire - Rob Rohn

PART III:
NEW STANDARDS

During the winter of 1964-65, Leo Grillmair and Hans Gmoser realized the attraction of the Bugaboos and its sporting potential. They also recognized the sheer genius and capabilities of what the helicopter could offer as a ski lift.

Machines could now provide man with another access to the Bugaboos. With the help of Jim Davies, a masterful mountain chopper pilot from Banff, they initiated skiers to one of the world's most exclusive ski areas. In the next decade those who had never heard of the Bugaboos because of its mountaineering reputation would now learn of it through its newly developed skiing potential.

In the climbing world of course, the Bugaboos were already well known and became for many rock climbers, one of the major stops in the circuit. Though no individual climber would be singled out as the most outstanding Bugaboo achiever, there would be, during the following 15 years, many individuals whose skills and efforts would far exceed those of past climbers. The new breed of climber would be characterized by many new facets: chalk bags, nuts and gymnastics. In the late sixties many of the newer climbers on the scene were gymnastics experts and from them, two significant developments evolved. Dick Williams, a Shawangunk climber and parallel bar champion, developed a new "swinging for holds" technique. The idea of three positive holds on the mountain was out the window. Dynamic moves for out-of-reach holds would push the limits of free climbing far beyond what had been thought possible.

With the gymnasts came the chalk bags. Dangling from their waists, climbers employ chalk to dry their sweat covered fingers and obtain a better grip on the extreme faces being attempted. Whether chalk is a psychological boost or a definite advantage in hard climbing it is difficult to say, but today's hard men might feel naked without their chalk bags.

A further advent of the late sixties was the increased use of nuts and cam devices for protection as opposed to pitons and bolts. Bolting has long been a controversial issue in climbing circles. Frank Smythe's arguments, and the controversial first ascent of Mt. Brussels in Canada's Rockies, as well as Yvon Chouinard's infamous Summit article, "Are Bolts Being Placed by Too Many Unqualified Climbers?", have led to the demise of bolting in most climbing situations. Climbs that had in the past required bolting are most often done without. Free climbing standards have advanced to the stage where many routes, even those requiring bolts, are being done completely free. Protection, it seems, has become the only requirement for using pitons.

Over the years, the use of pitons caused the deterioration of many routes to the point where pitons could not be driven and holds were crumbling. In Britain the situation on more travelled routes was particularly serious, thus the advent of machine nuts and more recently, specifically fabricated cams. Nuts and cams are far easier to use, lighter to carry, eliminate the need for a piton

The Howsers and Pigeon Spire from Bugaboo-Snowpatch col - J.F. Garden

hammer, and above all, do not damage the rock environment.

These new developments have led to the even higher climbing standards that now prevail. The California decimal grade 5.0 was pushed to 5.10 and beyond during the 1970's and winter ascents have become part of the new quest. Yvon Chouinard became the foremost mentor of ice climbing. He advocated a new style in the late sixties and early seventies, based on equipment which he modified for the job. Adapting crampons, ice-axes and ice-hammers to the special needs of ice climbing, waterfall ice became the most recent challenge. Routes that are frozen could be overcome in a fraction of the time required during the normal season. New ice routes, as well as winter ascents were now more than feasible, they were done!

Bugaboo Glacier tongue, 1985 - J.F. Garden

Bugaboo flowers - J.F. Garden

103

Pigeon and the Howser Spires at twilight - J.F. Garden

CHAPTER THIRTEEN:
Old and New Faces

Since 1910, when the Bugaboos first began to attract climbers, until 1966, a time span of 56 years, all of the peaks and many of the walls of the Bugaboos were climbed. However, even in 1966 there were numerous new routes and variations on the spires which yet remained unscaled.

The aesthetic south face of Snowpatch Spire succumbed finally, on July 21 and 22, 1966. As Conrad Kain remarked many years earlier, Snowpatch presents awesome walls from all angles. No Bugaboo face presented a more awesome aspect than this, but Richard C. Williams, John Hudson and Ants Leemets, V.M.C.[1] found the formula for victory.

From their camp at Cooper's Boulder, a musically inspired threesome scrambled up the lower reaches of Snowpatch after a leisurely 7 a.m. start. By noon they were into straight forward climbing of mixed fifth and sixth class work and had reached the top of the prominent buttress in the center of the face. With the musical accompaniment of his companions, Ants Leemets led up a jam-crack following the lower of a pair of diagonal cracks past two overhangs, using direct aid and ending up in a sling belay. Leads were then alternated; Dick up a triangular overhang, John working left on the face to a larger inside corner which arched upwards to form an overhang.

A difficult lead by Ants over dirt-filled cracks with strenuous piton work led to a small ledge which, though extremely crowded, became home for the night. The night was warm, the bivouac reasonably comfortable and July 22 dawned with a beautiful sunrise on the ranges. A 6 a.m. start was made up easy direct aid, then difficult piton work which went up jam-cracks leading to a sloping ledge. Bad weather began creeping in, but thoughts were concentrated on the best route possibilities. While ascending left to a ledge and up several more crack systems, hail began to pelt down. After some nervous moments on loose rock, another short traverse, a chimney with a chockstone, and two more crack systems, the first of the false summits was attained.

Snowpatch Spire from the southwest showing the south face on the right and the west face on the left - J.F. Garden

Wondering where the summit was, the threesome scrambled up and around and over, finally finding the top. Down the west face they rappelled to the snowfields, jubilant with success but needing the rest and relaxation that they knew Boulder Camp offered.[2]

Climbers heading for the Bugaboos continued to pursue the challenges of the big granite walls, creating a legend, as it were. A legend with an ethos surrounding the Bugaboo name and the names of those who climbed there. Virgin faces were yet to be climbed and as the equipment of the sport developed and the technique of the climbers advanced, the Bugaboo legend expanded with more firsts.

On August 5, 1967 climbers Peter Zvengrowksi, Gay Campbell and Bill Knowler completed a new route on the northwest face of Howser Spire. Their route lay up the two snowfields enclosed by the north ridge and west buttress of the face. From Bill's pass they made their way to the base of the 2500 foot face, then proceeded with an interesting rock and ice climb requiring direct aid only on one pitch near the summit. Bivouac was made after that pitch, but the following morning the summit was reached after three more leads.[3]

On August 9, Galen Rowell and Fred Beckey completed a new direct West Face route on Snowpatch Spire. After looking hard at a direct route to the true south summit of Snowpatch, Rowell and Beckey decided one afternoon to begin the attempt. On August 6 they left ropes in place for 300 feet, then had to sit out two days of rain before returning.

Before sunrise on August 9 they were back to their highest point expecting much more difficult climbing than the fifth class that it was. In fact the going was so good that bivouac gear was left behind in expectation of doing the route in the day. The final pitches were done in the glow of sunset, the nine pitches requiring some 95 pitons, half of which were used in direct aid.[4]

The final grand achievement of the 1960's had to be the second ascent of Beckey's east face route on Snowpatch, unclimbed in 10 years. Brian Green-

Snowpatch Spire, south face - J.F. Garden

wood, whose greatest achievement to date was on Mt. Temple's North Face in 1966, set out in July 1969 with John Moss, to repeat Beckey's success. Remarkably, Greenwood and Moss climbed the face in two days, with one bivouac under the big overhang. The first effort to the bivouac was almost all artificial climbing, but after that it was mostly free climbing to the summit.[5]

West face of the Howser Towers - U. Veideman

Beckey and Rowell climbed the couloir directly below the south summit of Snowpatch on this west face - James B. Maitre

It was obvious that climbing had advanced in the 10 years since Beckey's first ascent, but it was also possible that Fred Beckey was far ahead of his time in the climbing world of 1959. Chrome alloy pitons, aluminum chocks, better (Kernmantle) ropes, jumars, all came in the years since 1959. Prusiking 150 feet or more on an overhanging wall with manila prusik slings was a great struggle when compared to the ease of jumars. There is just no comparison in the speed and effort it now takes. When Beckey first did Snowpatch, moss had to be cleaned from the cracks before pitons could be driven. Following parties never needed to spend time cleaning or looking for piton placements as the spots were now obvious. On some routes free climbing has become possible because of the cleaner route. Has climbing then, actually advanced? Could it be that any advances are a result of better equipment?

View northward from the summit of Snowpatch Spire, Bugaboo Spire on the right - Roger W. Laurilla

The west face of the North Howser Tower rises direct in one massive central pillar of slabby granite to the summit of the highest point on the Howser Towers. This central pillar was, in 1970, a classic unclimbed route of Yosemite standards on an alpine peak susceptible to the whims of nature. It hosts a climate where the life and death of a climber may hang on the balance of a storm. On August 1 and 2, 1970, Chris Jones, Archie Simpson and Oliver Woolcock made a climb of the south-west face of North Howser Tower from a camp on the spur beneath the Central Howser Tower. They went up the hanging glacier and out onto the southwest face via a ledge which connected with a viable crack system to the top. This climb, though hardly the big daddy, showed them the direct west face route and gave Chris Jones much to think about over the winter months.

The intrigue took hold and Galen Rowell and Chris Jones returned to the Bugaboos in 1971 specifically to do the climb. Tony Qamar was talked into joining them. Waking early on the morning of July 28, snow was flying in their faces. When the weather cleared in the afternoon they took a closer look at the proposal and the following morning they were off, the overall difficulties of the climb somewhat less than expected.

With perfect weather and good going, their progress was a day ahead of their calculations. Expecting worse, the climb was somewhat of a let down. The next day there was a marked difference with the climbing a 5.7 or better.

"Our Yosemite experience paid off as we seemed to devour each succeeding pitch with cold-blooded efficiency," wrote Chris Jones. "It was hard climbing, some dozen pitches being 5.8 or higher, but all free save for 30 feet; we kept right on storming up."[1]

The Howser Towers from the northwest. In this view the size of the North Tower's western buttress can be seen. Jones, Qamar and Rowell climbed directly up that obvious buttress in 1971 - Scott Flavelle

After one pitch was led, the second man would jumar up to lead the next pitch and the third man would clean the pitons, and so on up the wall. On the thirty-fourth lead, the summit was reached just as the sun set. The cheers of a party on nearby Bugaboo Spire were heartfelt thanks and heightened the occasion immensely.

"True, it had not been as demanding as we had expected, yet it was probably the first Grade VI in the Interior Ranges on what is most likely the greatest granite face in the Interior," (Grade VI 5.9 A2) Jones wrote.[2]

1971 was full of activity in the Bugaboos. As well as the new route on Howser climbed by Chris Jones; Yvon Chouinard, Doug Tompkins and Pete Carman placed a new route up the east face of Snowpatch direct to the north summit. In this spectacular three day effort, aid was predominant.

Chris Jones and Jeff Lowe teamed up to do the southwest face of Snowpatch, but they found the rock quality on their two day climb not up to usual Bugaboo standards. Brian Greenwood and George Homer placed a new route on the right side of Snowpatch's west face which ended up on the southwest ridge.

Ted Davies and Pat Derouin followed the Greenwood-Homer route, then went straight up in a direct line to the top.

And in a surprisingly excellent climb, Ted Davies, Pat Derouin and Ian Rowe made a spectacular effort on the northeast corner of Snowpatch. They climbed it almost entirely free, up to 5.9 standard, even though many who had considered the route thought it would require a great deal of aid. A storm forced them off 300 feet below the summit, but it is highly likely that they had by then joined the summit ridge route.

In 1972 The Minaret, the obvious pillar on the southwest corner of South Howser Tower was ascended. (Grade VI 5.8 A3) Gerry Rogan and Jon Jones made this classic climb on Howser in August. They spent two days preparing the route from a camp below the South Tower. Then they got down to business, though progress was limited as at first they started out as a party of four. Bivouac that first

night was on a ledge with room for two, with the others suspended in hammocks. The night was warm.

Next morning, the climb proceeded well until one of the party dropped a jumar. The climb then began to bog down. Equipment and food were in too short supply for a big aid climb so it was back to the base of the Minaret for more supplies. Drawing straws to decide who should continue the attempt on the Minaret, Gerry Rogan and Jon Jones lost (or won?) and found themselves quite alone. Jones describes his feelings the night prior to the ascent.

"It was an extremely strange feeling which crept over me the next night. Rob, Judy and Marge had left us to go back to Butlin's. Gerry and I sat in the bivi at the bottom of the route just looking up at that magnificently sculptured tower. It was so quiet, unusually quiet. Not much wind, no animals or birds, no falling rock. Nobody around. A strange feeling of isolation gripped both of us."[3]

The next day they were off up the mountain.

"Soon we were up to our high point and things were going well. The day passed quickly. Still nailing in the same crack line, we found a small bivi ledge seven pitches up, got settled, and then fixed another pitch before packing it in. It had been a good day and we had plenty of food and water with us. I think both of us started to feel we were getting somewhere at last."[4]

Again the second day passed by quickly with more and more free climbing showing up.

"Gerry led up to the large overhangs which we thought might pose problems — not so, a gangway led straight through them. A pleasant easy angled corner pitch led up to a break leading right. We must be close now."[5]

Bivouacing on a ledge that sloped at about 40 degrees, Jones lost his sleeping bag to the depths below. The weather closed in around them as they huddled under a plastic sheet, heels in aid slings.

"The bivouac site was transformed into a big plastic observation bubble through which we could see all this lightning in the distance. Fortunately the storms kept off us that night."[6]

South Tower of the Howsers and on the right, the Minaret -
J.F. Garden

On the last day, with storms surrounding, they made the final push to the summit. The last three pitches were made in rain and hail and shortly after, while sorting out gear, their two companions of the first efforts arrived on the summit and accompanied them down to the comforts of camp.

In 1973, two Yosemite climbers arrived in the Bugaboos amid violent winds and lightning storms. Their intent was to place a route up the west face of North Howser Tower just left of the one done by Rowell, Jones and Qamar in '71.

When the weather finally cleared, Hugh Burton and Mike Irvine chose their line, and began climbing on obvious cracks that led some 800 feet up the face. They initially experienced varied free climbing up cracks and ramps to a large ledge beneath an obvious chimney, then after some distance, retreated to the large ledge and spent the night in bivouac. They were visited through the night by the ever-present snafflehounds of Bugaboo fame.

Burton wrote, "You feel a little incompetent, slowly struggling up the wall with all this gear while these furry little members are running circles around you. Unroped 5.11 with no boots."[7]

The following day, with good weather holding, the route led up excellent cracks over a snowpatch and on up the final tower. Up some free and some aid pitches, the base of the long face crack was reached. Some four and a half pitches were secured on that crack which gradually widened to three inches. Hammocks were secured for the night in an incredible bivouac of desolate beauty and serenity. Next morning, nailing upward on an excellent crack, several eagles were seen circling the towers in lazy flight. Into overhangs, Burton and Irvine worked some difficult aid sections as the weather began to deteriorate. A night of rain and snow was passed inside their wall tent.

On the last day the storm abated, the summit ridge was gained in two more beautiful leads. Before they could reach the summit peak lightning and hail forced serious consideration of immediate evacuation.

"Lightning cracks up all around," Burton wrote. "It hails furiously for half an hour and we huddled half sheltered by a huge block. A pretty dangerous perch – an easy target for lightning, so we decided to get moving. Off the other side of the ridge it drops 800 feet to a long 60 degree ice slope with rock cliffs at the bottom. Beautiful, we don't go that way – no crampons either. That leaves one choice, the west ridge. So we start rapping."[8]

After 10 rappels they reached the base of the rock but there they remained for yet another night, battered by furious winds and hail, lightning exploding all around.

"By morning things have calmed down," described Burton. "We start rapping down the mixed ground. Snow, ice, rock. Ten more 150 foot raps and we finally hit the glacier at the bottom. We stagger back to camp and collapse in an exhausted heap."[9]

They were five and a half days on the mountain, a route achievement of tremendous perseverence (Grade VI 5.9 A2) which Burton and Irvine aptly named Warrior.

In 1974, on August 4, 5 and 6, Mike Jefferson, Dennis Saunders and John Shervais established another route on the east face of Snowpatch (Grade VI 5.9 A2) which they named Deus ex Machina. The route began with a 5.9, off-width crack a few hundred feet north of the Chouinard direct route to the north summit. A bivouac in rain and hail

Pigeon, Snowpatch and Bugaboo Spires in the fall - Roger W. Laurilla

dampened spirits, but otherwise the route proved straightforward though exposed.

Also, on the right side of Snowpatch is a remarkably-placed route called the Tom Egan Memorial Route. (Grade VI 5.9 or 10 A4) It is here that some of the more fantastic Bugaboo climbing has been done in recent years.

Snowpatch was finally climbed in winter by Heiri Perk and Walter Renner in 1975. They required a bivouac on the summit. This remarkable climb was the first winter ascent of any of the Bugaboo Spires.

Considering the climbing feats achieved in the Bugaboos, especially during the decade of the 1970's, it was hard for most climbers to imagine what future exploits were left to consider. All indications point to advances in the areas of winter ascents, ice climbing, and free climbing. But will these accomplishments come so easily? In the Bugaboos, there are of course, no guarantees.

During the summer of 1978 two Canadians from the west coast, Daryl Hatten and John Simpson, arrived among the famous granite spires. Their endeavors led to the heights of Snowpatch Spire and a climb called the "Tom Egan Memorial Route," so named by Daryl after a climbing friend who died in Yosemite. John Simpson's reminiscences of the climb provide us with a firsthand account of that adventure.

"It was an amazing feeling: a strange mixture of wonder and fear. Wonder because I know that no one had ever been on this smooth sheet of granite in the millions of years that it has existed. Fear because the granite went beyond the vertical, arching out over the glacier several hundred feet below.

The only feature interrupting the smooth granite wall was a crack which dropped away, tapering to a thin grey line in the sunlit rock below. I dangled from metal wedges seated in this crack, acutely aware of the lack of footholds and handholds. I began to question the sanity of my situation, the folly I had entered upon in climbing this barren rock wall.

A tug on the rope around my waist broke my reverie. I looked up to see my friend, Daryl Hatten, climbing upward and outward along that same lonely crack.

Several days earlier, Daryl and I had been standing on the Bugaboo Glacier, awed by the spires towering around us. We had scanned the maze of cracks and chimneys for possible routes. Daryl's eye was caught by the solitary crack in a steep headwall near the Northeast corner of the East face of Snowpatch. We spent the rest of that afternoon

walking over the glacier, piecing together the route from different angles. It seemed that a few short pitches of free climbing would lead us to the base of an overhanging wall. The long crack would then carry us up the wall and onto the upper third of the face. This latter five hundred feet of rock was broken by cracks and chimneys which appeared to lead to the top of the Northeast corner of the peak.

As we put together a mental map of the cracks on the face, our excitement grew. The route looked intriguing, the weather was clear and a friend of ours had unwittingly abandoned his wall rack in the hut.

Later that evening, we scavenged what we needed from Carl's gear. His useful small and medium angle pitons disappeared into our growing pile of water bottles, nuts and bolts, warm clothes and food. Darkness found the clutter disappearing into a bulging haul sac and two climbers lying down for their last comfortable night. From my sleeping bag I looked out over the ice fall to the shadow of the Hound's Tooth. Stars filled the sky in a way that can never be seen except in the wild. Behind me, I could feel Snowpatch standing dark and quiet over the hut. I wondered if the mountain would be receptive to two insignificant humans scratching their way up the granite face. Or would we be rejected in no uncertain terms by difficulties as yet unseen.

Daryl and I had considerably different experience in big wall climbing. Daryl was a veteran with a good understanding of the force of gravity and a wealth of climbing skill stored within his solid frame. I was about to set off on my second big wall climb. Ignorance was bliss, so I fell asleep easily.

We woke to a warm sun and a noisy hut – two signs of a late start. After a lazy breakfast we realized that we were losing our credibility as eager alpine climbers. Uncomfortably full of Coyote pancakes (the manufacturer dubbed them 'a howling success') we set off up the moraines with the idea of climbing to the base of the headwall that day. As the moraines rolled into the glacier, our climb unfolded into the sky. The face rose sharply from

the bright snow, its dark cracks splitting the warm sunlit rock. At the end of our walk across the glacier we were stopped by a small bergschrund which formed a moat between the ice and the face. Daryl passed me a rope end and I started the climb with a tentative hop over the fissure onto some holds in a blocky corner. After a short pitch of gentle free climbing amongst the blocks, I stopped to massage my expanding breakfast. Daryl soon took my attention from my 'howling' cakes as he swung leftwards, leading a straight forward aid traverse. After getting reacquainted with my jumars, I cleaned the gear from the traverse and set off up the next corner pitch. I climbed slowly, excavating amongst the beautiful clumps of moss that had taken hundreds of years to grow on some of the holds. At the end of a long pitch, I reached the beginning of the overhanging headwall. Here Daryl and I made the decision to call it a day and go down to the hut for another comfortable night.

Early the next morning we ascended the ropes and organized our gear for the headwall crack. We decided that it was not worth having three ropes on the wall so, in the interests of lightening the haul sac, I demonstrated the art of throwing a rope into a bergschrund. Daryl was not impressed. He decided he would lead the headwall.

Our predictions of thin aid climbing were unfounded. The long crack started by taking knife blades to the eye, then widened slowly to take several nuts and angle pitons. As Daryl made quick work of the leads, the mountain sun started to warm us. Rays bounced up from the glacier and bounced off the east face of Bugaboo until we were comfortable in shirts.

We were not the only wildlife enjoying the sun that day – bees were swarming all over the rock and in and out of the crack along its length. By the time we reached the top of the headwall our initial fears of the bees had worn off and we were used to sharing the rock with them.

With the end of the headwall, the gently overhanging sheet of granite rolled into vertical rock and another, larger crack was born a few feet to our left. A small, but convenient ledge linked the top

us, we decided that the top of this rock was a good place to spend the night. Daryl found that he could curl up on one part of the rock – I found that I could sit wedged on another. Overproof rum helped us to mould to our niches. We had a fitful sleep curled up in the chimney on the mountain.

By morning, I was eager to shake out my shivering muscles so I set off up the chimney on a quest for sun. Daryl breakfasted in the chimney and belayed me while I wondered when I should break out to the exposure of the open rock and warmth. When Daryl joined me, he found that he recognized our position on his mental map of the face so he directed our route as we climbed through the remaining maze of cracks towards the top.

After a morning of gentle mixed climbing we pulled onto the shoulder of the Northeast corner of Snowpatch. This was the end of our route. The climb had gone without a hitch and the weather had been with us. The mountain had relented and allowed us to enjoy the vertical wall and the satisfaction of completing a new route. Tired and happy, we feasted in the sun, sitting on the edge of a huge spike of granite. A long, long stone's throw below a sea of ice curved around us then rolled into the valley to feed the rivers that led seaward. From our perch in the soaring blue air, we could see no limits to our friendly earth."

In June of 1979, a route on the South Howser Tower was established in a solo ice climb by Jon Krakauer. This route followed the distinctive ice filled gully on the South Tower's right-hand side and was appropriately named the Ice Hose. It consisted of 800 feet of ice at a pitch of 70 degrees or more. The ice continued nearly all the way to the top of the peak and made for good time, though the last 80 feet became rock and rotten cornice snow which finished the route off in an exciting fashion.

of the long narrow crack with the start of the new crack. The new crack was offwidth as it was not quite large enough for the human body to slide into sideways. It looked unpleasant so we broke for lunch on the ledge to think on it!

It was a beautiful place to stop. Our legs dangled in space over hundreds of feet of rock while breadcrumbs drifted unimpeded to the glacier below. The only detraction from the lunch was a slight queasiness in my stomach. As the pancakes had passed safely to lower levels, I knew that the feeling resulted from apprehension of the pending route up the off-width crack.

Steeling myself, I left the ledge to thrash on the lips of the fissure half in its mouth and half out. Occasionally, I could find small cracks if I reached into the back of the fissure. From these cracks I could dangle on pitons and nuts. Using a strange mixture of dangel and thrash, I reached the top of the offwidth in a blur of huffing and puffing.

The rest of the day was a more pleasant mix of free and aid climbing up to a wide dark chimney which was plugged by a large flat topped rock and backed with snow. As we had no hammocks with

Howser Spires, west face - J.F. Garden

All but the last section was third class ice climbing and descent was made by rappelling down the east face. In "Climbing" magazine Krakauer describes the route: ". . . sustained every foot of the way – one of the few alpine ice climbs that's steep enough so that waterfall climbers don't get bored with it, yet mellow enough to cruise on."[1]

In the summer of 1980, Canadian climber Mike Tschipper made very notable ascents in the Bugaboos, ascents done previously but of special interest because they had been aid routes which Tschipper and his companions completed free. Though originally rated as 5.9 A2, the route that Tschipper and Ward Robinson completed on North Howser Tower's west face had been pushed to a 5.10 A1 with few points of aid remaining. This was to be the first free climb on this direct west face route and was also the first Canadian ascent of the face.

After an initial abortive attempt a week earlier, Tschipper and Robinson began their climb late one August day as the weather was clearing.

"The lower portion of the climb was quite enjoyable for several pitches then rapidly deteriorated in vertical riverbed," wrote Tschipper.[2]

Using fixed ropes left on their earlier attempt, the team reached their bivouac spot for the night on the buttress which marks the halfway point of the route.

"The next morning turned out to be one of the largest, most sustained, and tiring days of my life," describes Tschipper. "Beautiful hand cracks took us into an ice and snow choked gully. Ice filled cracks and chimneys were climbed until progress was stopped by a house sized chockstone in the chimney. From here we swung out and around to the left hand side of the gully. Continuous 5.8 to 5.9 cracks led us up and left to a broken corner system. We continued climbing till alpenglow and the summit ridge were in sight, knowing we had it in the bag. In all, the route was quite good and not technically beyond many climbers, although rock-fall is a problem."[3]

The second 5.10 free climb Tschipper made that August of 1980 was on the classic and only route on Bugaboo Spire's east face. This was the route put up by Ed Cooper in 1960, and though climbed many times since, the last 30 feet of aid was still to be climbed free. Tom Gibson and Mike Tschipper became the first climbers to complete the free ascent of this face.

"All that remained as of 1979 was a blank 30 foot section of bolts. The only feasible way in which it was thought it would go free was to the right 10 feet. This usually wet section proved to be relatively dry the day we were there," outlined Tschipper. "Thin face moves made the bolt placements difficult but in the end it all went at 5.10 + ."[4] The east face of Bugaboo Spire was now a free climb.

Greg Cameron on the bolt ladder, east face of Bugaboo Spire - Rob Rohn

Pages 120-121
South and Central Howser Towers beyond the Bugaboo-Snowpatch col - J.F. Garden

Harbouring thoughts of an expedition to Patagonia and curious to know what granite big walls were all about in a cold and harsh regime, Phil Hein and Scott Flavelle conceived the idea of climbing the Beckey-Chouinard route on South Howser Tower in winter. Scott had previously planned the winter ascent with another fellow-climber in January of 1979 when the temperature was forty below zero. They opted for frozen waterfall climbing instead.

During the summer of 1980, while in the Cirque of the Unclimbables, Phil and Scott discussed the climb tentatively for December, but with work coming up (both are guides with Canadian Mountain Holidays) those plans too, fell through.

Then on Phil's impetus they managed to coincide their time off, met in the Mad Trapper Pub in Golden, B.C. and drove into the Bobbie Burns Lodge where the next morning they were airlifted by helicopter to the base of the west side of the Howsers. It was March 15, 1981, the weather had been good for the two weeks previous, the mountain was dry and clear of loose snow. Scott's personal recollections recount the adventure that took place...

"...The pilot was a cowboy type who motors along in his machine, cigarette and toothpick hanging askew; aghast at the absurdities into which he propels his passengers. He shook his head and looked at us strangely. Perhaps hoping to deter us, he flew around the mountain, though we only wanted to be transported to its base. The manager of the lodge, an older Swiss guide who was flying with us, knew why we wanted to go – but you would never catch him there either!

"Finally landing, the pilot's only words were, 'nice knowin' ya' and away they went in a cloud of snow and a thumping whir. Here we were way back on the west side of the Howsers, in the middle of nowhere. Coming from a heli-ski lodge by chopper you do not feel like you are out in the wilderness – until suddenly the chopper is gone. Not until then do you realize it is not coming back. We were

committed and did not expect to see or hear from anyone for six days.

"With harnesses on and packs full of equipment we walked down to the start of the climb. It seemed a decadent way to arrive, not having to sweat for hours to reach the base of the mountain.

"Then we began, roped climbing and hauling from the start. We climbed eight pitches that first day. It was quite dry, not too cold. We did not need to wear gloves in the sun, but with double boots and super-gaiters on, the climbing was awkward. The double boots were not good in narrow cracks and there weren't really any holds so it was very strenuous on the arms unless you reverted to aid climbing. Rock climbing shoes are more standard on Bugaboo granite.

"With about an hour of daylight remaining and no obvious bivouacs above, we cleared snow from a ledge on the side of the mountain, just large

enough to accommodate our little wall tent. We fixed one pitch above our camp for tomorrow's start and then rappelled down.

"Phil and I hadn't seen each other for some time so we were razzing each other throughout the evening, the way some friends can do in fun. Ensconced in our sleeping bags after dinner we settled in to sleep, but there was an annoying sound of shuffling nylon disturbing the quiet. I assumed Phil was causing the disturbance and he thought it was me. Trying to sleep, Phil suddenly asks what I am doing. Back and forth we harangued, but eventually fell asleep.

"Rising next morning we grabbed for the food bag and its contents spilled. The side of the tent and the bottom of the bag had both been eaten

Phil Hein at the start of the first winter ascent of the South Howser Tower - Scott Flavelle

West face of the Howser Towers from the southwest - Scott Flavelle

through by a rodent – a snafflehound. We had a good laugh about the situation after our thoughts during the night. It seemed, much to our amazement, that packrats existed on these rock spires no matter what the weather or the season!"

That night the weather turned foul. Though the sun had shone brightly the day before, it never appeared on the second day. Snow fell lightly, a lot of sluff and spindrift wafted down the cracks and crannies of the west face. After the climb Scott discovered that the storm existed only on the mountain, skiers in the area had had fairly clear skies the whole week!

Climbing the 250 foot dihedral above their first bivouac, Scott describes the climb.

". . .We encountered good climbing despite conditions in the long dihedral, but it was colder now so we had to rely more on aid climbing to get us over difficult spots. Snow was plastered into all the cracks causing a hindrance in finding belay anchors. Spindrift was continually coming down. At one point, while climbing some dihedrals watching snow streaming down through the rock, I had to place a two-inch bong. The running snow was deflected out into my face, so I had to pound it in blindly, snow pouring down my neck. Once up we traversed to a sandy ledge at the base of the Great White Headwall which was the normal bivouac on the mountain.

"Our tent was secured in the bottom of a dihedral. During the night spindrift funnelled down onto the tent, collapsing Phils' end. Phil slept little. The next morning everything was in a shambles and wet. Ropes were rimed and stiff, much of our gear buried. Our third day on the mountain was going to be more leisurely. We needed to reorganize.

Phil Hein on pitch one, South Howser Tower - Scott Flavelle

The second bivouac, Phil Hein and the wall tent
- Scott Flavelle

Pitch eleven - Scott Flavelle

Spindrift blowing down near the top of pitch seven
- Scott Flavelle

"Up above the bivouac was the Great White Headwall. The two very long pitches we did that day were all aid. The regular route goes straight up through a chimney but we realized we would have to try something else as the chimney was choked with snow and slippery. With the cracks in the chimney too big to put in any sort of protection, we opted for the face left of the chimney — discontinuous cracks which proved very time-consuming.

"The sun shone that day and while we climbed on the headwall our gear was drying on the ledges below. By late afternoon we had fixed our two ropes and rappelled back to our bivouac."

That third evening the helicopter appeared...

"...We heard the helicopter coming. We stood out on our little veranda sipping on a cup of tea, watching. On board, concerned and curious, were our fellow heli-ski guides and a well known Swiss photographer.

"It was a strange moment. They waved from the security of the helicopter only 10 minutes away from dinner and a bed. We waved from our tiny ledge perched high on the west side of the Howsers, our two ropes fixed to the rock above, beckoning us. What will we find up there?"

Jumaring up the fixed ropes they had left in place on the Great White Headwall, Scott and Phil started their fourth day on the mountain.

In the upper end of the chimney, which had by now turned into a gully, they had their closest call. The rocks in the gully were looser than normal. While Scott was climbing he dislodged a rock the size of a melon, narrowly missing Phil.

Phil Hein on pitch fourteen - Scott Flavelle

Scott Flavelle on the pendulum pitch, taken by Phil Hein - Scott Flavelle

Cleaning the route on the 16th pitch - Scott Flavelle

Jumaring on the fourth day - Scott Flavelle

From a notch above the chimney Phil led towards some pitons that he had spotted high above, but then the route did not seem so obvious at all. He fiddled around with the pitch, consuming much time and effort, ran short of rope and came down.

They decided they would have to try something different to get where they wanted to be. On Scott's turn he led out a long pendulum to the right reaching a series of cracks which led straight up the face. He wanted to climb quite a long way up these cracks without putting in any protection. That way Phil would not have to rappel down and then climb up, cleaning the route. Leap-frogging protection like that still involves having two pieces in, just to be safe. The face was most enjoyable in the warm afternoon sun, but all too soon the day was over.

Phil Hein on the 22nd pitch - Scott Flavelle

Near the top of the pitch, as light was fading, they encountered their only ice climbing. In order to reach a belay, Scott had to chip holds in the icy slab of rock with an alpine hammer. After that Phil was able to lead on to a snowpatch bathed in bright moonlight, clinging to the side of the mountain. There he dug out a small ledge for the tent and anchored for the night...

"The sky was crystal clear the next morning. Above was the summit ridge. It was just a matter of finding the easiest way up. We traversed an easy but exposed snow slope across the face until we could go straight up to the ridge.

"Although the summit stay was too short, we were happy to be at the top. We could see all the other spires, and many of the big peaks in the Rockies.

"Getting down was supposed to be easy, but with all the winter's cornices we could not find the standard rappel route. We had to make a new one. Five rappels later we were down the face and over the 'schrund. A few hundred meters away were our skis and soon we were on our way to Bugaboo Lodge.

"In retrospect, the climb was definitely the experience we had wanted. It turned out to be the stepping stone to bigger, colder and harder rock walls in alpine settings."

Summit cornice, South Howser Tower - Scott Flavelle

Scott Flavelle on the summit of the South Howser Tower, March 19, 1981, taken by Phil Hein - Scott Flavelle

Jumping the bergschrund - Scott Flavelle

CHAPTER SEVENTEEN:
Granite

Defined geologically as a crystalline rock of quartz, orthoclase feldspar, and mica or horn-blende; granite is often synonymous with big wall climbing in mountaineering circles. The peaks of the Mont Blanc Massif, Patagonia, Yosemite and the Bugaboos, to name a few, are all composed of this solid crystalline rock which tends to provide some of the best (and safest) and most pleasurable wall climbing of all. Hard climbers tend to prefer the pleasures of granite, and so areas such as Yosemite have become a haven for those who wish to climb "beyond the vertical."

Throughout the summer of 1981 Tom Gibson and Rob Rohn travelled across the continent in search of granite. The thought of climbing on such perfect rock fired their imaginations and their bodies. Their quest, as Rob Rohn relates, brought them back eventually to Canada and the Bugaboos.

"In the spring, while the northern peaks remained encased in winter snows, we fled to California to the monolithic walls of Yosemite, to Tahquitz and Suicide Rocks. There, on steep geometrically perfect cracks we trained bodies and minds, absorbing the feel of jagged crystals on toughening hands, the squeak of rubber on minute edges, the exhilaration of pulling up on shaky finger locks, finding our fingers had seemingly learned to sprout roots for anchors.

"As summer approached we migrated north. My dream was to apply those high technical standards to the mountains back home, to climb long difficult Yosemite-like routes on the alpine spires of the Selkirks and Purcells.

"We flew into the south side of the Adamant Range in July, its weathered rock walls all but ignored by climbers. The dark towers were enshrouded in mist and cloud, enticing yet repulsive for though the walls and buttresses were reminiscent of Yosemite, the weather was not. Incessant rains on the tent fly and violent flapping of our kitchen tarp in the winds that raked our camp tested our determination and patience.

Snowpatch, west face - J.F. Garden

"When the weather finally broke we found everything we had hoped for: the sweeping buttresses of Ironman and the Turret, rippled granite, cold and grey. Tom and I were determined to free-climb wherever possible, climbing solely on the natural features of the rock, using ropes and anchors only as a backup in case of a fall, much like a gymnast's safety net. It was a style we found much more satisfying than aid-climbing, where one moves upward on anchors placed in cracks and flakes, sometimes even resorting to drilled holes and bolts.

"After three weeks in the area the weather was still brilliant and it was time to move on. I had unfinished business in the Bugaboos and now was the time, the sunshine wouldn't last forever. With a sense of urgency and 80 pound packs we hiked over to the north side of the range, to Fairy Meadow and down a trail infested with devil's club, back to my ancient Volvo. There, judging by the footprints, it had aroused a lot of interest from the local bears.

"Despite a concerted effort by ourselves and the Volvo, we did not make it to the Mad Trapper in Golden, B.C. before closing time. And the next day being Sunday, we were forced to piece together our provisions for the Bugs from the meager selection in the only open convenience store in town.

"Now back on home ground, we took the familiar trail up to Boulder Camp. How many magical days had I experienced on these gleaming spires? And how many indescribably-boring days in the hut, trapped by endless rainfall. The contrasts of a mountaineer's life.

"We found lots of friends in the cabin. The international climbing community is remarkably close-knit. You travel thousands of miles and keep running into the same faces.

"Early next morning we were alone again, plodding up the well-beaten track to the Bugaboo-Snowpatch col and across onto the Vowell Glacier below the west face of Snowpatch Spire. I had spotted this line years before, a system of brilliant white cracks and corners shooting directly for the north summit.

"I'd made a half-hearted attempt to climb it the previous summer with two other friends, Greg Cameron and Dean Lister. It had been a cold, misty day and the first really difficult pitch, a thin crack in a steep corner, had taken forever to lead. But the dirt and moss had already been forgotten, overshadowed by the awesome, drastically-leaning crack above, much too steep for even the hardiest lichen. The crack was an awkward size, too wide to secure a finger, yet not wide enough for a whole hand. It reminded me of a short climb in Yosemite called Crimson Cringe. I cringed at the prospect of a pitch that difficult and strenuous way up here.

"I've always found in this sort of situation the best thing is to avoid thinking about what you're getting yourself into and just dive in. I quickly arranged the rack of equipment and set off as Tom belayed, paying out the rope as I climbed. It was immediately obvious that this was going to be just as difficult as I'd feared. There was not even a ripple in the steely-smooth granite to provide a foothold, so I stuffed hands into the flared crack. Feeling very insecure, I stopped every 10 or 15 feet to place a protection anchor in the crack and clip in the rope so that it would catch me in a fall.

"As forearms started to burn with strain, I was tempted to grab one of the anchors in order to sit back on the rope and rest. It would be so easy to do. But by the arbitrary rules of the game that we had set for ourselves, this would be an admission of defeat. We'd come to free-climb wherever possible, and I knew that here, though at my limit, I would have to endure.

"The crack seemed to stretch forever, without so much as a foothold for a rest. With the last dregs of energy spent, the corner was broken by a tiny ledge. I pulled onto this oasis in the vertical desert with only a couple of feet of rope to spare. I sank back in a stupor.

"Following, Tom looked as haggard as I felt. Our meager bottle of water had already been drained and with it my energy and drive. Conversation was limited to a few dry mumbles. Our only motivation to continue was the knowledge that if we didn't get to the top, we'd just have to come back and do it all over again. Reluctantly Tom shouldered the rack and set off.

"The crack widened considerably to six inches – too wide for hands or fists and not wide enough to crawl inside. Tom wriggled his way up this to the top of the corner using techniques perfected on warm California granite. A difficult traverse on delicate flakes to more steep cracks landed him on another ledge 150 feet higher.

"And still the difficulty and angle of the rock were unrelenting. More vertical cracks required jamming fingers and toes into perfect, speckled granite. This should be fun, exhilarating I thought. But we'd overdosed on fun. Now all I wanted was to reach the top so that I could get back down to the glacial streams, a tantalizing mirage 1500 feet below.

"Then I was on a ledge, the north summit of Snowpatch Spire was only a few feet above on easy terrain. The final scramble seemed anticlimactic. Bodies and minds were thrashed and wanted only to return to the flat world below.

"Long tedious rappels followed before we could reach the glacier below. Our concentration was strained both by exhaustion and dehydration. We couldn't yet afford to relax our guard. Mercifully our feet touched soft snow and we dashed to a nearby glacial pool to slake our thirst. The icy water numbed our brains, but revitalized us. We gazed up at our route and let out loud victory cries that echoed from the surrounding walls.

"There followed a rapid slide down from the Bugaboo-Snowpatch col and the rubble-strewn glacier back to Boulder Camp. The day ended in the hut with lots of stories and endless cups of hot drinks that our bodies absorbed like great insatiable sponges. At last there came the deep, self-satisfied sleep that follows a great day in the hills.

"Shouldn't we have been satisfied after such an obvious success? Summer was drawing to a close and we decided that while we were on a roll we'd throw the dice one more time.

Tom Gibson on the Direct North Summit route, west face of Snowpatch Spire - Rob Rohn

132

Crux pitch, Direct North Summit, west face of Snowpatch Spire — Rob Rohn

"After a rest day we were off to an early start, this time with two water bottles in our pack. The south face of Snowpatch Spire presents that peak's most impressive profile. It was first climbed in 1966 using much direct aid. But a casual comment from a friend, who had repeated the route and remarked that it might go free, had clicked in my mind and I'd filed it under future projects.

"A lot of moderate scrambling led to the vertical wall where the real climbing began. A hundred feet higher a pair of thin, parallel cracks, like giant misplaced ski tracks, shot up the wall, promising technical and strenuous climbing. It was Tom's

lead. I lazed in the warm sunshine, belaying him as he methodically worked out the puzzle. He slotted fingers in subtle pockets in the crack, tip-toed up tiny gleaming crystals and danced gracefully up this vertical stage.

"The crack split two small overhangs, then thinned so that it accepted only fingertips. The climbing was getting really hard. Suddenly I was awakened from my overly-relaxed state by a jerk on the rope. Tom, unable to solve a particularly difficult move before his arms gave out, had taken a short fall past his last piece of protection. Undaunted, and with minimal cursing, he climbed

back to his high point and powered on up to the ledge that marked the end of the pitch.

"A short overhanging corner and a long traverse left led to the final obstacle between us and the summit. Here the regular route followed a leaning corner of indistinct cracks that didn't look as if they would succumb readily to our free climbing efforts. A steep flake to the right looked strenuous but feasible. The only question was whether we would be able to get back to the easier ground of the regular route from the top of the variation. There was only one way to find out.

Snowpatch Spire, south face - J.F. Garden

Tom Gibson on the 5.11 finger crack, south face of Snowpatch Spire - Rob Rohn

"It was Tom's lead again and he forged upward. With feet plastered against a wall and arms pulling outward on the edge of a crack, he laybacked up to the top of a vertical flake. Here the rock started to overhang, barring upward progress. The only possibility was a traverse back left to the top of the difficult corner that seemed almost close enough to leap to.

"Tom made tentative attempts at the traverse, searching for the right combination of knobs and edges, returning each time to a semi-rest at the flake. Then he went for a dynamic swing from straining fingers to hook a distant foothold and once gained found better handholds leading to broken, easy ground.

"The final moderate pitches floated by until there was no more uphill and we stood on the summit. A handshake and a slap on the back. It had been a good climb and a good season.

"The next two days passed quietly down at Boulder Camp. We relaxed in the sunshine and joked with friends, content to contemplate the summits from below. A certain goal had been attained and ambitions satisfied; for the moment anyway.

"And as we plunged down the trail to the car on a cool, overcast morning I knew that the lure of the vertical world would draw me back again to the rock and ice of these jagged granite spires."

South face of Snowpatch Spire — Rob Rohn

Heli-skiers in Northpost Couloir - J.F. Garden

EPILOGUE

Modern day challenges remaining in the Bugaboos may seem insignificant compared to those facing the original explorers. First ascents of peaks, then first ascents of seemingly-impossible walls were theirs. Now all that remains is to repeat past feats in better style and to master winter ascents. Are not those challenges far greater than the original? Perhaps. But then, how is it possible to do better than the masters such as Kain, Beckey, Cooper and Chouinard? Are not conditions perhaps more difficult during winter climbs than when pioneering routes were climbed on the best of days?

Whatever the challenges, they are obviously still there because year after year climbers are attracted to pit their skills and resolve against the Bugaboo granite. The area is a hive of activity all year save in the fall and early winter. Considered too late in the season for climbing and too soon for the heli-skiing for which the Bugaboos are now famous, late fall is the only time of the year when there is not an excess of people at Boulder Camp or Bugaboo Lodge.

Now known as the Bugaboo Recreation Area, the region was placed under the protection of the British Columbia government in 1969 as the Bugaboo Glacier Provincial Park. The Conrad Kain hut, constructed by the Alpine Club of Canada in 1972, is now operated by the friendly hut custodians of the Provincial Park Service.

Bugaboo Lodge, built in 1967 by Hans Gmoser and Leo Grillmair of Canadian Mountain Holidays, is now the mecca for downhill skiers. Europeans and Americans especially seem to be enamoured with the area and tend to return year after year to CMH's ski holiday tours.

The Bugaboo Spires themselves have not changed at all since Conrad Kain's first climbs of 1916, though the glaciers have melted considerably. What has changed is the ease of access and subsequently the attraction of the area to sportsmen. Certainly, much has changed in the civilized world and more and more people seek the pleasures and escape of mountain solitudes. The pressure of the crowds has indeed been felt in the Bugaboos, those solitudes becoming less utopian. With the press of more and more people, however, comes the aware-

Bugaboo Lodge - U. Veideman

ness and concern necessary to encourage the preservation of nature. Perhaps with the fame and international renown of the Bugaboos, an everlasting guarantee of protection and preservation just may be assured.

A three-mile hike from the end of a logging road now leads to Boulder Camp and the Conrad Kain hut. The trail itself restricts the area to ambitious hikers and mountain climbers. The Conrad Kain hut is a luxurious haven compared to previous camps under the huge glacial boulders, once the principal domiciles of visiting alpinists. The hut is cared for by two attendants from the Parks Service, and a fee is collected for its maintenance and improvement.

Most summers I visit the Bugaboos early in August and an example of the activities in the area was demonstrated on an enjoyable day in 1982. It was a perfect day for photography.

Sunrise is very often the most notable and spec-

tacular time of day as the Bugaboo peaks face eastward. After photographing that event my companion and I travelled up the Bugaboo Glacier to the base of Snowpatch's south face and looked across the ice-filled amphitheatre to the great sloping slabs of Pigeon Spire and its east facing profile. On Ed Cooper's classic route there were two climbers intent on making the friction traverse at the top of the slabs. With fascination we watched their progress for some time.

Following a wind ridge up the upper reaches of the Bugaboo Glacier we eventually arrived at the base of Pigeon Spire's west ridge, the normal route up the mountain. From the ridge a grand vista unfolds with the Howser Towers on the right and the ridges of the Selkirks beyond. Two parties of climbers had just completed the climb of Pigeon and among them were two ladies who had never climbed a mountain and in fact never believed they could.

Climbers on the east face of Bugaboo Spire — J.F. Garden

The party we watched had to follow that example. They ran out of the pins necessary to do the pendulum pitch above the wall and couldn't therefore reach the south ridge of Snowpatch. Their rappel was vertical, and free much of the way down. For them and for us, it was back to the haven of the Kain hut, and an evening with interesting people and entertaining tales of the mountains.

One story which came to light recently is of Peter Croft's day in the Bugaboos. In a frenzy of activity he climbed the Beckey-Chouinard route on South Howser with a partner, then carried on solo up the McCarthy route on the west face of Snowpatch, over to the McTech arête on Crescent and then did the Northeast ridge of Bugaboo Spire, all in a single day![1] Impossible you say! Perhaps for most of us. However with modern techniques and the freedom of climbing unencumbered, physical conditioning

All afternoon, clouds were tearing off the high peaks which topped off the vertical walls of the Howsers. Down the Vowell Glacier one was confronted with the back faces of both Bugaboo Spire and Snowpatch which are spectacularly vertical. Our route was across the névé to the col between the two spires, a footworn path across the smooth upper surfaces of the Vowell Glacier. Descending the Bugaboo-Snowpatch col, a treacherous effort until across the bergschrund which gapes open below the rocks, we enjoyed a boot ski all the way down to the open snowfields below. Above, to the north is the east face of Bugaboo Spire. A party of climbers on their second day were seen working into the bolt section of Cooper's classic route. To the south and above the col is the smooth light brown shoulder of Snowpatch, a ridge of rock that seems extremely holdless.

On the east face of Snowpatch there were two parties, one on the central face and one on the vertical Tom Egan Memorial Route. The Tom Egan is a great sandy coloured slab of granite which sweeps up vertically into the blue. On the entire slab there is only one apparent line, a small continuous crack leading upward, nearly impossible to discern except for bits of red climbing slings left abandoned where rappels were necessary in retreat.

Mountain Sorrel - J.F. Garden

and the right mental state, plus good weather — why not? Peter's day reflects the kind of climbing frenzy or overindulgence that the rock scenery of the Bugaboos can induce. It seems that anything might be possible in the Bugaboos.

Standing high and isolated amidst the tumble of peaks which comprise the Purcell Mountains, the Bugaboos have a distinctive appearance. Granite spires bound by ice stand alone like headstones in a geologic graveyard. Their profile attracted the curiosity of the original explorers, but what is it that now attracts the modern explorers?

Stories of climbing adventure, success and failure, names and events; tales of perfect granite, atrocious weather and snafflehounds; accounts of people who have been to the Bugaboos: big name climbers, young adventurers, photographers. All who come share an adventure. Tales are told of those adventures.

The spires stand alone in dark jutting outlines against the sky, a story in themselves. A story which relates back many millions of years in the earth's history. More recently, however, the story involves people who have made the Bugaboo Spires a fascinating place.

Legendary figures such as Conrad Kain, Fred Beckey, Ed Cooper, Hans Gmoser and many others have given the Bugaboos an enthralling history as exciting as any in the annals of climbing and adventure. Their names have become a vital part of the Bugaboo legend.

Bugaboo Spire and the west face of Snowpatch - J.F. Garden

Moon over Snowpatch Spire - J.F. Garden

Crescent Spire in evening light - J.F. Garden

APPENDIX A

Climbing Grades:

Example: NCCS VI 5.8 A3

NCCS – refers to the National Climbing Classification System

VI – roman numerals refer to the overall difficulty of the route, I through VI, which includes factors such as the elevation of the peak, the vertical rise involved, time involved for the climb, difficulty of hardest pitch, difficulties of retreat, descent and overall strenuousness of the climb.

    I - half a day
   II - most of a day
  III - a long day
  IV - a long day with a possible bivouac
   V - two full days with one bivouac required
  VI - multi-day climb

5.8 – arabic number describes the difficulty of the limiting or crux pitch, which when reaching 5.0 means the use of pitons for protection with this being a continuously expanding grade system, advancing to 5.10, 5.11, etc., as free climbing standards are pushed.

A3 – refers to the degree of aid required on the hardest of pitches.

APPENDIX B

The Bugaboo Spires — First Ascents

Name	Elevation		First Ascent
Anniversary Peak	9650′	(2912 m)	F.A. Aug. 1916 - H.O. Frind, A.H. & E.L. MacCarthy, G. & J. Vincent, C. Kain N. Face Aug. 1959 - E. Cooper, A. Gran, R. Sadowy
Brenta Spire	9650′	(2912 m)	F.A. July 1938 - L. Coveney, S.B. Hendricks, P. Olton, P. Prescott, M. Schnellbacher
Bugaboo Spire	10450′	(3185 m)	F.A. Aug. 1916 - A.H. & E.L. MacCarthy, J. Vincent, C. Kain (Kain route) W. Face Aug. 1959 - E. Cooper, E. Pigou N. Face Aug. 1960 - L. Kor, C. Suhl E. Face Aug. 1960 - E. Cooper, A. Gran
Crescent Spire	9350′	(2854 m)	F.A. June 1933 - J.M. Thorington, C. Kain
Eastpost Spire	8850′	(2700 m)	F.A. Aug. 1938 - E. Cromwell, F.S. North
Flattop Peak	10050′	(3064 m)	F.A. Aug. 1930 - E. Cromwell, P. Kaufmann
Howser Peak	10150′	(3095 m)	F.A. Aug. 1916 - H.O. Frind, A.H. & E.L. MacCarthy, G. & J. Vincent, C. Kain
Howser Spires			N.S. Traverse Aug. 1965 - Y. Chouinard, J. Lang, E. Rayson, D. Tompkins
N. Tower	11150′	(3400 m)	F.A. Aug. 1916 - H.O. Frind, A.H. & E.L. MacCarthy, G. & J. Vincent, C. Kain W. Buttress Aug. 1963 - F. Beckey, B. Greenwood
C. Tower	10850′	(3308 m)	F.A. Aug. 1955 - G. Austin, D. Bernays, J. MacCarthy, J. Rupley
S. Tower	10850′	(3308 m)	F.A. Aug. 1941 - L. Anderson, H. Beckey, L. Boyer, T. Campbell W. Buttress Aug. 1961 - F. Beckey, Y. Chouinard
Marmolata	9950′	(3037 m)	F.A. Aug. 1930 - E. Cromwell, C. Kain, P. Kaufmann
Northpost Spire	9550′	(2915 m)	F.A. Aug. 1938 - D.P. & J.A. Richards
Pigeon Spire	10250′	(3125 m)	F.A. Aug. 1930 - E. Cromwell, P. Kaufmann N. Face July 1948 - F. Beckey, J. Heib, R. Widrig E. Face Aug. 1960 - E. Cooper, L. Kor
Snowpatch Spire	10050′	(3064 m)	F.A. Aug. 1940 - J. Arnold, R. Bedayn W. Face Aug. 1956 - H. Kraus, J. McCarthy E. Face Aug. 1959 - F. Beckey, H. Mather S. Face July 1966 - J. Hudson, A. Leemets, R. Williams

Bugaboo Spire and the Howser Towers above the Vowell Glacier
- Glen Boles

Bugaboo flower gardens - Roger W. Laurilla

GLOSSARY

Aid - the use of mechanical devices to ascend rock or ice faces.

Arête - a narrow mountain ridge that drops away on both sides.

Belay - the method of protecting a climber from above or below using the hands and body as friction on the climbing rope which is fastened to the climber.

Bergschrund or 'schrund - the line along which the tensile strength of the snow in a moving glacier is insufficient to overcome the inertia of its mass. It is generally reflected by a large crack or separation of snow near the base of a rock wall or mountain.

Bivouac - a term denoting a campsite on a ledge, notch, col or any other part of a mountain. Sometimes the climber is suspended in a hammock on a sheer wall by nothing other than bolts or pitons driven in the rock.

Bolts - metal spikes driven into holes drilled into a face of rock, may be expansion bolts or other types.

Bongs - large metal pegs usually made of aluminum or chrome alloy, with large holes cut in the metal to lighten its weight. Used in wide cracks where pitons are impractical.

Carabiners - an oval shaped metal ring with a spring gate on one side built to allow a rope to be clipped in. It has many uses in aid climbing and free climbing and as a safety device.

Chimney - a vertical crack or fissure in a mountain sometimes becoming a vertical tunnel.

Col - a notch or depression between peaks: a high pass.

Crampons - metal frame which attaches to the sole of climbing boots and which usually has 10 or 12 spikes on it to aid in climbing ice and snow.

Dihedral - refers to a vertical angle created by two faces or planes of rock which come together often providing the climber with a route of ascent.

Friends - a new innovation, it is a metal spring loaded cam device which is inserted in cracks or fissures: a person squeezes it so that it fits in, then releases the handle and the serrated cams hold in the rock and provide an anchor.

Gendarme - a rock pinnacle usually blocking the way along a ridge or arête.

Layback - a method of climbing a corner or slab where a vertical crack for handholds exists, but nothing other than friction or pressure holds the feet. The body is held by the pull of hands in the crack and push of feet against the rock, in other words the climber is laying back from the rock.

Massif - a geographical term denoting a large block of a mountain which may have a number of peaks or summits upon it.

Moraine - the debris and rock pushed along by a glacier or carried on top or on the side of a glacier, usually deposited when the ice melts.

Nuts (Chock-nuts) - a newer climbing device designed to be used in lieu of pitons. They are small octagonal, or square, or cam shaped pieces of metal which fit into cracks and can be used to protect a climber or for aid climbing. The idea came from chock-stones which are rocks jambed in cracks or chimneys of mountains.

Pitons - a metal spike or wedge which may be knife shaped or angled and of various sizes driven by a piton-hammer into cracks for protection and aid climbing. Now being replaced by nuts for environment and weight saving reasons.

Prusik - a means of climbing a rope using prusik slings, which wrap around a rope providing friction, the climber then stands in one prusik sling, moving a second sling up the rope for a higher stance. Named for Karl Prusik - a German physical fitness instructor. Now mechanical devices such as JUMARS with slings attached are used. These metal devices clamp onto the rope providing the necessary friction.

Rappel - a means of descending a mountain using a double rope where friction around the climber's body or through a mechanical device allows vertical descent of a mountain face. Abseil - roped down controlled.

Traverse - climbing horizontally across a face along ledges or cracks, or up one route and down another.

Pendulum Traverse - a rope is fastened high on a wall and then by swinging back and forth on the rope a climber reaches for a far hold or crack on a wall, which is otherwise impossible to reach.

Verglas - an ice layer covering a rock, usually very thin and hard caused by water running down a face or rock, freezing at night or in a storm.

Morning light on Snowpatch and Bugaboo Spires - J.F. Garden

NOTES

PART I

1. Doug Scott, Big Wall Climbing, Kaye and Ward, 1974, p. 24

Chapter One

1. Thomas G. Longstaff, This My Voyage, John Murray, London, 1950, p. 230.

2. In 1819 Wilmer C. Wells crossed a pass in the Purcells which was subsequently named Wells Pass and was later named Earl Grey Pass after one of Canada's Governor Generals. Wells later became an M.L.A. for the Windermere district and Minister of Public Works for the Province of British Columbia. Wilmer, B.C. was named in his honour.

3. Thomas G. Longstaff, "Across the Purcell Range of British Columbia", Geographical Journal 1911, p. 592.

4. Ibid, p. 593.

5. Ibid.

6. Hound's Tooth (Marmolata) 9,950 feet.

7. Snowpatch - 10,050 feet.

8. Pigeon Spire - 10,251 feet.

9. Thomas G. Longstaff, This My Voyage, John Murray, London 1950, p. 231.

10. Howser Towers - 11,150 feet.

11. Author's note: Devil's Club (Oplopanax horridum): beautiful large green leaves topping off thick stems four to ten feet tall, bristling with spines which are brittle and cause festering sores.

Chapter Two

1. Author's note: No. 1 - Pigeon Spire, No. 2 - Snowpatch, No. 3 - Bugaboo Spire.

2. Snowpatch - Bugaboo col.

3. Author's note: Pigeon Spire.

4. Howser Spires - 11,150 feet.

5. A.H. MacCarthy, "The Howser and Bugaboo Spires", Canadian Alpine Journal, VIII, p. 19.

6. Ibid., p. 21.

7. Ibid., p. 22.

8. Author's note: Bugaboo Spire.

9. A.H. MacCarthy, "The Howser and Bugaboo Spires", Canadian Alpine Journal, VIII, p. 26.

10. Ibid, p. 27.

11. Conrad Kain, "Reminiscences of Seven Summers in Canada", American Alpine Journal, Vol. 1, 1929-1932, pp. 293-294.

12. A.H. MacCarthy, "The Howser and Bugaboo Spires, Purcell Range", Canadian Alpine Journal, VIII, p. 27.

Chapter Three

1. Conrad Kain, "Reminiscences of Seven Summers in Canada", American Alpine Journal, Vol. 1, 1929-1932, p. 292.

2. Eaton Cromwell, "In the Bugaboo Group", American Alpine Journal, Vol. 1, 1929-1932, p. 297.

3. Ibid., p. 298.

4. Ibid., p. 299.

5. Conrad Kain, "Where the Clouds Can Go", edited by J. Monroe Thorington, The American Alpine Club, New York, 3rd edition 1979, p. 437.

PART II

1. Doug Scott, Big Wall Climbing, Kaye and Ward Ltd., London, 1974, p. 24.

Chapter Four

1. Percy T. Olton, Jr., "The Bugaboos", American Alpine Journal, Vol. 3, 1938, p. 295-297.

2. Raffi Bedayn, "A Bugaboo No Longer", American Alpine Journal, Vol. 4, p. 219.

3. Ibid., p. 221.

4. Ibid., p. 222.

5. Ibid.

6. Ibid., p. 223.

7. Ibid., p. 224.

8. Ibid.

9. Ibid.

10. Ibid.

Chapter Five

1. Lyman Boyer, "South Tower of Howser Spire", Canadian Alpine Journal, Vol. 28, p. 38.

2. Lloyd Anderson, "The Last of the Bugaboos", American Alpine Journal, Vol. 4, p. 421.

3. Lyman Boyer, "South Tower of Howser Spire", Canadian Alpine Journal, Vol. 28, p. 40.

4. Ibid., p. 41.

Chapter Six

1. Fred Beckey, "Pigeon Spire From the North", Canadian Alpine Journal, Vol. 32, p. 50.

2. Fred Beckey, "A Bugaboo Adventure", American Alpine Journal, Vol. 7, p. 135.

3. Ibid.

4. Fred Beckey, "Pigeon Spire From the North", Canadian Alpine Journal, Vol. 32, p. 51.

5. Ibid., p. 52.

6. Fred Beckey, "A Bugaboo Adventure", American Alpine Journal, Vol. 7, p. 136.

7. Ibid., p. 137.

8. Robin Hansen, "Lightning in the Bugaboos", Canadian Alpine Journal, Vol. 32, p. 133.

9. Ibid.

10. Ibid.

Snowpatch Spire at dusk — J.F. Garden

Chapter Seven

1. Chris Jones, <u>Climbing in North America</u>, Berkeley and Los Angeles, University of California Press, 1976, p. 236.

2. David Bernays, "The Central Howser Spire", <u>American Alpine Journal</u>, Vol. 10, p. 105.

3. Ibid., p. 106.

4. James P. McCarthy, "West Face of Snowpatch", <u>American Alpine Journal</u>, Vol. 10, p. 31.

5. Ibid., p. 32.

6. Roper and Steck, <u>Fifty Classic Climbs of North America</u>, Sierra Club Books, San Francisco, 1979, pp. 55-59.

Chapter Eight

1. Ed Cooper, "West Face of Bugaboo Spire", <u>Canadian Alpine Journal</u>, Vol. 43, p. 74.

2. Ibid., p. 75.

3. Fred Beckey relates, "in my book he did the South West face."

4. Fred Beckey writes, "we used these on the first pitch above the glacier (I think!). Never above, they were heavy and bulky of course."

5. Fred Beckey, "East Face Snowpatch Spire", <u>American Alpine Journal</u>, Vol. 12, p. 23.

Chapter Nine

1. Ed Cooper, "Bugaboo Spire East Face", <u>American Alpine Journal</u>, Vol. 12, p. 384.

2. Ibid.

3. Ibid.

4. Art Gran, "First Ascent of East Face, Bugaboo Spire", <u>Canadian Alpine Journal</u>, Vol. XLIV, p. 81.

5. Ed Cooper, "Bugaboo Spire East Face", <u>American Alpine Journal</u>, Vol. 12, p. 385.

6. Art Gran, "First Ascent of East Face, Bugaboo Spire", <u>Canadian Alpine Journal</u>, Vol. XLIV, p. 81.

7. Ed Cooper, "Bugaboo Spire East Face", <u>American Alpine Journal</u>, Vol. 12, p. 385.

8. Art Gran, "Other Notes", <u>Canadian Alpine Journal</u>, Vol. 44, p. 83.

9. Layton Kor, "First Ascent of Bugaboo-North Face", <u>Canadian Alpine Journal</u>, Vol. 44, p. 82.

10. Ed Cooper relates that Layton Kor was feeling quite poorly that day and perhaps may have consumed some bad food. Cooper on the contrary much enjoyed the climb and felt in great form.

11. Ed Cooper, "Pigeon Spire, East Face, Bugaboos", <u>American Alpine Journal</u>, Vol. 12.

Chapter Ten

1. Fred Beckey, "New Climbs in the Bugaboos", <u>Canadian Alpine Journal</u>, Vol. 45, p. 128.

2. Roper and Steck, <u>"Fifty Classic Climbs of North America"</u>, Sierra Club Books, San Francisco, 1979.

3. Fred Beckey, "West Face of the South Tower of Howser Spire", <u>American Alpine Journal</u>, Vol. 13, p. 59.

4. Fred Beckey, "New Climbs in the Bugaboos", <u>Canadian Alpine Journal</u>, Vol. 45, p. 128.

5. Fred Beckey, "West Face of the South Tower of Howser Spire", <u>American Alpine Journal</u>, Vol. 13, p. 59.

6. Ibid., p. 60

Bugaboo Spire at dusk – J.F. Garden

7. Fred Beckey, "New Climbs in the Bugaboos", Canadian Alpine Journal, Vol. 45, p. 127.

8. Ibid.

9. Ibid.

Chapter Eleven

1. Fred Beckey, "Howser Spire, West Face, Bugaboos", American Alpine Journal, Vol. 14, p. 198.

2. Ibid., p. 199.

Chapter Twelve

1. Chris Jones, Climbing in North America, University of California Press, Berkeley, 1976, p. 362.

2. Douglas R. Tompkins, "First Traverse of the Howser Spires, Bugaboos", American Alpine Journal, Vol. 15, p. 39.

3. Ibid.

4. Ibid.

PART III

Chapter Thirteen

1. Author's note: V.M.C. - Vulgarian Mountain Club.

2. John Hudson and Richard C. Williams, "The South Face of Snowpatch Spire", American Alpine Journal, Vol. 15.

3. Peter Zvengrowski, "North Howser Tower, Direct West Face", American Alpine Journal, Vol. 16.

4. Galen Rowell, "Snowpatch Spire, Direct West Face", American Alpine Journal, Vol. 16.

5. Brian Greenwood, "East Face, Snowpatch Spire", Canadian Alpine Journal, Vol. 54.

Chapter Fourteen

1. Chris Jones, "The West Face of North Howser Tower", Canadian Alpine Journal, Vol. 55, p. 3.

2. Ibid.

3. Jon Jones, "The Minaret, South Howser Tower", Canadian Alpine Journal, Vol. 56, p. 22.

4. Ibid., p. 23.

5. Ibid.

6. Jon Jones, "The Minaret, South Howser Tower", Canadian Alpine Journal, Vol. 56, p. 23.

7. Hugh Burton, "Warrior", Canadian Alpine Journal, Vol. 57, p. 8.

8. Ibid., p. 9.

9. Ibid.

Chapter Fifteen

1. Climbing, No. 54, May-June 1979, pp. 5-6.

2. Mike Tschipper, "North Howser Tower, West Face", Canadian Alpine Journal, Vol. 64, p. 83.

3. Ibid.

4. Mike Tschipper, "Bugaboo Spire, East Face", Canadian Alpine Journal, Vol. 64, p. 84.

Epilogue

1. Peter Croft, "Bugaboos, Place or State of Mind?", Canadian Alpine Journal, Vol. 67, pp. 18-19.

BIBLIOGRAPHY

Books:

Dowling, Phil, The Mountaineers, Famous Climbers in Canada, Hurtig Publishers, Edmonton, 1979.

Jones, Chris, Climbing in North America, University of California Press, Berkeley and Los Angeles, 1976.

Kain, Conrad, Where the Clouds Can Go, Edited by J. Monroe Thorington, 3rd ed., The American Alpine Club, New York, 1979.

Kruszyna, Robert and William L. Putnam, Climbers Guide to the Interior Ranges of British Columbia - South, 6th ed., The American Alpine Club and The Alpine Club of Canada, 1977.

Longstaff, Thomas G., This My Voyage, John Murray, London, 1950.

Roper, Steve and Allen Steck, Fifty Classic Climbs of North America, Sierra Club Books, San Francisco, 1979.

Scott, Doug, Big Wall Climbing, Kaye and Ward Ltd., London, 1974.

Periodicals:

Climbing Magazine, Bill Dunaway, Publisher, Aspen, Colorado, Published bi-monthly since May-June 1970.

Lake Windermere Valley Echo, Supplement of 1977, Invermere, British Columbia.

Bugaboo Spire at twilight - J.F. Garden

Alpenglow - Scott Flavelle

Journals:

Anderson, Lloyd, The Last of the Bugaboos, The American Alpine Journal, Vol. 4.

Beckey, Fred, Pigeon Spire From the North, Canadian Alpine Journal, Vol. XXXII.

Beckey, Fred, A Bugaboo Adventure, The American Alpine Journal, Vol. 7.

Beckey, Fred, East Face of Snowpatch Spire, The American Alpine Journal, Vol. 12.

Beckey, Fred, New Climbs in the Bugaboos, Canadian Alpine Journal, Vol. XLV.

Beckey, Fred, West Face of the South Tower of Howser Spire, The American Alpine Journal, Vol. 13.

Beckey, Fred, Howser Spire, West Face, Bugaboos, The American Alpine Journal, Vol. 14.

Beckey, Fred, Pigeon Spire, Southeast Face, The American Alpine Journal, Vol. 14.

Bedayn, Raffi, A Bugaboo No Longer, The American Alpine Journal, Vol. 4.

Bernays, David, The Central Howser Spire, The American Alpine Journal, Vol. 10.

Boyer, Lyman, South Tower of Howser Spire, Canadian Alpine Journal, Vol. XXVIII.

Burton, Hugh, Warrior, Canadian Alpine Journal, Vol. LVII.

Cooper, Ed, West Face of Bugaboo Spire, Canadian Alpine Journal, Vol. XLIII.

Cooper, Ed, Bugaboo Spire, East Face, The American Alpine Journal, Vol. 12.

Cooper, Ed, Pigeon Spire, East Face, Bugaboos, The American Alpine Journal, Vol. 12.

Croft, Peter, Bugaboos, Place or State of Mind?, Canadian Alpine Journal, Vol. 67.

Cromwell, Eaton, In the Bugaboo Group, The American Alpine Journal, Vol. 1.

Gran, Art, First Ascent of East Face, Bugaboo Spire, Canadian Alpine Journal, Vol. XLIV.

Gran, Art, Other Notes, Canadian Alpine Journal, Vol. XLIV.

Gran, Art, Snowpatch Spire, West Face, The American Alpine Journal, Vol. 13.

Greenwood, Brian, East Face, Snowpatch Spire, Canadian Alpine Journal, Vol. LIV.

Hansen, Robin, Lightning in the Bugaboos, Canadian Alpine Journal, Vol. XXXII.

Hudson, John and Richard C. Williams, The South Face of Snowpatch Spire, The American Alpine Journal, Vol. 15.

Jones, Chris, The West Face of North Howser Tower, Canadian Alpine Journal, Vol. LV.

Jones, Jon, The Minaret, South Howser Tower, Canadian Alpine Journal, Vol. LVI.

Kain, Conrad, Reminiscences of Seven Summers in Canada, The American Alpine Journal, Vol. 1.

Kor, Layton, First Ascent of Bugaboo - North Face, Canadian Alpine Journal, Vol. XLIV.

Longstaff, Thomas G., Across the Purcell Range of British Columbia, Geographical Journal, 1911.

MacCarthy, Albert H., The Howser and Bugaboo Spires, Canadian Alpine Journal, Vol. VIII.

McCarthy, James P., West Face of Snowpatch, The American Alpine Journal, Vol. 10.

Olton, Percy T., Jr., The Bugaboos, The American Alpine Journal, Vol. 3.

Richards, Mr. and Mrs. I.A., First Ascent of Northpost Spire, The American Alpine Journal, Vol. 3.

Rowell, Galen, Snowpatch Spire, Direct West Face, The American Alpine Journal, Vol. 16.

Schnellbacher, Marguerite, West of Spillimacheen, Canadian Alpine Journal, Vol. XXVI.

Schnellbacher, Marguerite, Fist Ascent of Brenta Spire, Canadian Alpine Journal, Vol. XXVI.

Shervais, John, Snowpatch Spire, East Face, Deus ex Machina Route, Bugaboos, The American Alpine Journal, Vol. 20.

Thorington, J. Monroe, The Bugaboo-Howser Watershed, The American Alpine Journal, Vol. 2.

Tompkins, Douglas R., First Traverse of the Howser Spires, Bugaboos, The American Alpine Journal, Vol. 15.

Tschipper, Mike, North Howser Tower, West Face, Canadian Alpine Journal, Vol. LXIV.

Tschipper, Mike, Bugaboo Spire, East Face, Canadian Alpine Journal, Vol. LXIV.

Zvengrowski, Peter, North Howser Tower, Direct West Face, The American Alpine Journal, Vol. 16.

Crevasses on the Bugaboo Glacier - J.F. Garden

H. Uro
April. 1992
Matison